Active ALGEBRA

Algebra I

Guided Practice Book

Name _____

Teacher Created Materials
PUBLISHING

Authors
Carol Edgar and Jamie Robin

Editor
Karie Feldner Gladis, M.S.Ed.

Associate Editor
Heather Brashear, M.S.

Assistant Editor
Torrey Maloof

Editorial Assistant
Kathryn R. Kiley

Editorial Director

Emily R. Smith, M.A.Ed.

Editor-in-Chief
Sharon Coan, M.S.Ed.

Editorial Manager
Gisela Lee, M.A.

Production Manager
Peter Pulido

Creative Director
Lee Aucoin

Publisher
Rachelle Cracchiolo, M.S.Ed.

Illustration Manager/Designer
Timothy J. Bradley

Designer
Neri Garcia

Imaging
Phil Garcia   Debbie Brown
Misty Shaw   Don Tran

Foreword Author
Dr. Debi Mink, Executive Director of the
    Teacher Education Center, Miami-Dade County
    Public Schools, Miami, Florida

Introduction Author
Pamela H. Dase, M.A.Ed., Retired Teacher,
    Certified National T³ Instructor, Powell, Ohio

Mathematics Consultants
Lori Barker, Georgetown, Texas
Donna Erdman, M.Ed., Spring, Texas
Brenda Bourque, Vidor, Texas
Missy Garcia-Stevens, Fredricksburg, Texas

Teacher Created Materials Publishing
5301 Oceanus Drive
Huntington Beach, California 92649
http://www.tcmpub.com
© 2007 Teacher Created Materials Publishing

Table of Contents

Mathematics Chart 5

Unit 1: Algebraic Expressions and Integers

Adding Integers 1 7

Adding Integers 2 8

Multiplying and Dividing Integers 9

Group Activity 1. 10

Group Activity 2. 11

Collecting Like Terms. 12

Distributing and Collecting 13

Writing Equations Packet 14

Unit 2: Linear Equations

Cups and Chips 1. 24

Cups and Chips 2. 25

Cups and Chips 3. 26

Solving Equations 1 27

Solving Equations 2. 28

Adding and Subtracting Fractions 30

Multiplying and Dividing Fractions 31

Algebra Applications with Angles 32

Mixed Fractions 34

Literal Equations 1 36

Literal Equations 2. 37

Writing Equations Review 38

Literal Equations 3. 42

Unit 3: Probability, Percent, and Proportion

Percent of Region Packet 43

Percent of Region Notes 47

Percent 1 48

Probability 50

Percent 2 52

Percents Review. 54

Quick Percents. .56

Proportions 1 57

Measurement Review 60

Proportions 2 64

Probability, Percent, and
Proportion Review. 67

Unit 4: Graphing

Solving for y Part 1 71

Solving for y Part 2 72

Functions, Domains, and Ranges 73

Graphing Mid-Unit Review 75

Measurement Review (Mid-Unit Graphing) . .77

Adding Integers (for Slope) 81

Slope 1 82

Slope 2 84

Slope 3 86

Slope 4 88

Scatter Plots Packet 90

Solving for y and Slope Review 94

Fractions Review 96

Writing Equations of Lines 98

Graphing 1 100

Graphing 2 102

Parameter Changes Packet 104

Parameter Changes Review 109

Graphing Unit Review 1 110

Measurement Review (Graphing Unit) 112

Graphing Memorization Sheet. 116

Graphing Unit Review 2 118

Unit 5: Inequalities

One-Variable Inequalities 120

Solving Compound Inequalities ("ands") . . .122

Solving Compound Inequalities ("ors"). 124

Compound Inequalities Review. 126

Absolute Value Inequalities
(Special Cases). 128

Unit 6: Writing Systems of Equations & Semester Review

Making Additive Inverses 130

Writing Systems of Equations 1 131

Writing Systems of Equations 2 134

Writing Systems of Equations 3 137

Systems of Equations Unit Review 1 139

Measurement Review (Systems Unit) 141

Systems of Equations Unit Review 2 145

Semester Review 1 (Graphing) 147

Semester Review 2 (Writing
One-Variable Equations) 150

Semester Review 3 (Mixed Objectives) 152

Semester Review 4 (Graphing) 154

Semester Review 5 (Writing
Two-Variable Equations) 156

Unit 7: Polynomials

Adding and Multiplying Monomials 1 158

Adding and Multiplying Monomials 2 159

Adding Polynomials Using Algebra Tiles 160

Adding and Multiplying Monomials 3 161

Perimeter of Triangles 162

Angle Measures 163

Area and Perimeter 164

Area of a Shaded Region 165

Geometry Review (Polynomials Unit) 166

Polynomials Unit Review 1 167

Polynomials Unit Review 2 170

Unit 8: Factoring

Dimensions of Rectangles 173

Geometry Review (Factoring Unit) 175

Factoring Unit Review 1 177

Factoring Unit Review 2 179

Applications 1 181

Applications 2 183

Applications 3 185

Applications 4 187

Unit 9: Radicals and Quadratics

Applications 5 189

Applications 6 191

Simplifying Radicals 1 193

Simplifying Radicals 2 194

Applications 7 195

Area and Perimeter with Radicals 197

Applications 8 199

Geometry Review (Radicals and
Quadratics Unit) 201

Simplifying Quadratic Answers 204

Quadratics Unit Review 205

Unit 10: Rational Expressions & Semester Review

Simplifying Rational Expressions 1 208

Simplifying Rational Expressions 2 209

Simplifying Rational Expressions 3 210

Simplifying Rational Expressions 4 211

Fractions Review 212

Rational Expressions Mid-Unit Review 214

Adding and Subtracting
Rational Expressions 216

Rational Expressions Unit Review 1 217

Rational Expressions Unit Review 2 219

Algebra I Second Semester Exam Review . . .221

Appendices

Appendix A: Graphing Calculator Practice . .230

Appendix B: Glossary of Algebra Terms 237

Mathematics Chart

AREA	circle	$A = \pi r^2$
	rectangle	$A = lw \qquad$ or $\qquad A = bh$
	trapezoid	$A = \frac{1}{2}(b_1 + b_2)h \quad$ or $\quad A = \dfrac{(b_1 + b_2)h}{2}$
	triangle	$A = \frac{1}{2}bh \qquad$ or $\qquad A = \dfrac{bh}{2}$
CIRCUMFERENCE	circle	$C = 2\pi r \qquad$ or $\qquad C = \pi d$
PERIMETER	rectangle	$P = 2l + 2w \qquad$ or $\qquad P = 2(l + w)$
SURFACE AREA	cone (lateral)	$S = \pi rl$
	cone (total)	$S = \pi rl + \pi r^2 \qquad$ or $\qquad S = \pi r(l + r)$
	cube	$S = 6s^2$
	cylinder (lateral)	$S = 2\pi rh$
	cylinder (total)	$S = 2\pi rh + 2\pi r^2 \quad$ or $\quad S = 2\pi r(h + r)$
	sphere	$S = 4\pi r^2$
VOLUME Note: B represents the area of the base of the solid figure.	prism or cylinder	$V = Bh$
	pyramid or cone	$V = \frac{1}{3}Bh \qquad$ or $\qquad V = \dfrac{Bh}{3}$
	sphere	$V = \frac{4}{3}\pi r^3 \qquad$ or $\qquad V = \dfrac{4\pi r^3}{3}$
Distance Formula		$d = \sqrt{(x_2 - x_1)^2 + (y_2 - y_1)^2}$
Midpoint Formula		$\left(\dfrac{x_1 + x_2}{2}, \ \dfrac{y_1 + y_2}{2}\right)$
Pi (π)		$\pi \approx 3.14 \qquad$ or $\qquad \pi \approx \dfrac{22}{7}$
Point-Slope Form of an Equation		$y - y_1 = m(x - x_1)$
Pythagorean Theorem		$a^2 + b^2 = c^2$
Quadratic Formula		$x = \dfrac{-b \pm \sqrt{b^2 - 4ac}}{2a}$
Simple Interest Formula		$I = prt$
Slope of a Line		$m = \dfrac{y_2 - y_1}{x_2 - x_1}$
Slope-Intercept Form of an Equation		$y = mx + b$

Mathematics Chart *(cont.)*

CAPACITY AND VOLUME	
Metric	1 liter = 1,000 milliliters
Customary	1 gallon = 4 quarts 1 gallon = 128 ounces 1 quart = 2 pints 1 pint = 2 cups 1 cup = 8 ounces

LENGTH	
Metric	1 centimeter = 10 millimeters 1 meter = 100 centimeters 1 kilometer = 1,000 meters
Customary	1 foot = 12 inches 1 yard = 3 feet 1 mile = 5,280 feet 1 mile = 1,760 yards

MASS AND WEIGHT	
Metric	1 gram = 1,000 milligrams 1 kilogram = 1,000 grams
Customary	1 pound = 16 ounces 1 ton = 2,000 pounds

TIME	
	1 minute = 60 seconds 1 hour = 60 minutes 1 day = 24 hours 1 week = 7 days 1 year = 365 days 1 year = 52 weeks 1 year = 12 months

Teacher Created Materials
PUBLISHING

#10623—Active Algebra—Algebra I, Guided Practice Book

Name _____

Adding Integers 1

Directions: Calculate.

1. $-1 + 6 =$ _____

2. $-2 - 3 =$ _____

3. $4 - 2 =$ _____

4. $4 - 6 =$ _____

5. $2 - 1 =$ _____

6. $3 + 2 =$ _____

7. $4 - 1 =$ _____

8. $-3 + 2 =$ _____

9. $-4 - 1 =$ _____

10. $-1 - 1 =$ _____

11. $-2 + 3 =$ _____

12. $-4 - 2 =$ _____

13. $-2 - 3 =$ _____

14. $6 - 5 =$ _____

15. $3 - 4 =$ _____

16. $-4 + 9 =$ _____

17. $-2 - 2 =$ _____

18. $-5 - 1 =$ _____

19. $1 - 3 =$ _____

20. $2 - 2 =$ _____

21. $3 - 1 =$ _____

22. $1 - 3 =$ _____

23. $-2 - 4 =$ _____

24. $-3 + 5 =$ _____

25. $6 - 2 =$ _____

26. $5 - 6 =$ _____

27. $3 - 4 =$ _____

28. $-3 - 4 =$ _____

29. $-1 + 4 =$ _____

30. $-3 - 5 =$ _____

31. $-3 + 6 =$ _____

32. $8 - 7 =$ _____

Name _____

Adding Integers 2

Directions: Calculate.

1. $5 - 9 =$ _____

2. $3 + 4 =$ _____

3. $-6 - 1 =$ _____

4. $-3 + 4 =$ _____

5. $-2 - 1 =$ _____

6. $-3 + 8 =$ _____

7. $8 - 1 =$ _____

8. $-2 + 4 =$ _____

9. $-6 - 2 =$ _____

10. $-3 - 5 =$ _____

11. $-1 - 1 =$ _____

12. $-6 + 5 =$ _____

13. $-8 + 3 =$ _____

14. $6 - 10 =$ _____

15. $-8 - 2 =$ _____

16. $-3 + 4 =$ _____

17. $-5 - 8 =$ _____

18. $-3 + 5 =$ _____

19. $-3 + (-5)$ _____

20. $-6 + 4 =$ _____

21. $-4 - 2 =$ _____

22. $8 - 7 =$ _____

23. $-5 - 3 =$ _____

24. $3 - 8 =$ _____

25. $2 - 10 =$ _____

26. $9 - 12 =$ _____

27. $-4 - 5 =$ _____

28. $-3 + 10 =$ _____

29. $-5 - 1 =$ _____

30. $-7 - 3 =$ _____

31. $-2 - 1 =$ _____

32. $-2 + 7 =$ _____

Teacher Created Materials PUBLISHING

#10623—Active Algebra—Algebra I, Guided Practice Book

Name _____

Multiplying and Dividing Integers

Directions: Calculate.

1. $-12 \div 3 =$ _____

2. $6(-4) =$ _____

3. $-8(-5) =$ _____

4. $\dfrac{-24}{6} =$ _____

5. $-2(-1)(-1) =$ _____

6. $-20 \div 2 =$ _____

7. $\dfrac{-3}{5} \cdot \dfrac{2}{3} =$ _____

8. $-6(-3) =$ _____

9. $-10(-3)(-2) =$ _____

10. $\dfrac{-40}{8} =$ _____

11. $-32 \div 4 =$ _____

12. $-1(-1)(-1)(-1)(-1) =$ _____

13. $\dfrac{-100}{-10} =$ _____

14. $-6(7) =$ _____

15. $-300 \div 10 =$ _____

16. $\dfrac{-2}{3} \div \dfrac{1}{6} =$ _____

17. $-5(-3)(-2) =$ _____

18. $\dfrac{-3}{4} \cdot \dfrac{2}{3} =$ _____

19. $-3(5)(-2) =$ _____

20. $\dfrac{-60}{-5} =$ _____

21. $-48 \div 6 =$ _____

22. $72 \div -9 =$ _____

23. $-5(6) =$ _____

24. $\dfrac{-2}{5} \div \dfrac{1}{10} =$ _____

25. $-6 \cdot \dfrac{2}{3} =$ _____

26. $(-1.2)(3.4) =$ _____

27. $\dfrac{-3}{4} \cdot \dfrac{1}{5} =$ _____

28. $\dfrac{1}{3} \div (\dfrac{-2}{5}) =$ _____

29. $(-2)(-3) + (4)(-8) =$ _____

30. $(3)(-6) - 18 =$ _____

Names _____

Group Activity 1

Directions: Simplify.

1. $-3 + 8 =$ _____
2. $-7(-4) =$ _____
3. $6 - 10 =$ _____
4. $11 - 5 =$ _____
5. $-2 - 6 =$ _____
6. $14 - 18 =$ _____
7. $-24 \div 3 =$ _____
8. $\dfrac{16}{-8} =$ _____
9. $4 \div 0 =$ _____
10. $6 \div 0 =$ _____
11. $-2 + 5 =$ _____
12. $6 - 8 =$ _____
13. $-3 - 5 =$ _____
14. $-2(5) =$ _____
15. $-6 \cdot -9 =$ _____
16. $4 - 8 =$ _____
17. $-6 - 10 =$ _____
18. $-3(-7) =$ _____
19. $-4 + 10 =$ _____
20. $-4 - 8 =$ _____
21. $-6 \div 2 =$ _____
22. $-32 \div -8 =$ _____
23. $16 - 20 =$ _____
24. $-3 - 4 =$ _____
25. $-2 - 2 =$ _____
26. $0 - 8 =$ _____
27. $-3(-4)(2) =$ _____
28. $(-2)(-3)(-6) =$ _____
29. $-4 \cdot 3 + 5 =$ _____
30. $\dfrac{1}{3} \cdot \dfrac{-2}{5} =$ _____
31. $\dfrac{-3}{4} \cdot \dfrac{-6}{7} =$ _____

32. $\dfrac{-3}{5} \div \dfrac{2}{5} =$ _____
33. $-6(-3) - 20 =$ _____
34. $\dfrac{-4}{5} \div \dfrac{-2}{3} =$ _____
35. $\dfrac{-6 - 2}{-3 + 7} =$ _____
36. $-2 - 7 =$ _____
37. $-2(-7) =$ _____
38. $6 - 13 =$ _____
39. $6 - 2 =$ _____
40. $\dfrac{-28}{-7} =$ _____
41. $-6(-2) + (-3)(7) =$ _____
42. $-6 \div (-3) + 7 - 10 =$ _____
43. $-10(3) + 4(-2) =$ _____
44. $-8 - 3 =$ _____
45. $-9(6)(-3) =$ _____
46. $\dfrac{108}{-12} =$ _____
47. $-2 - 3 =$ _____
48. $-6 + 3 =$ _____
49. $-4 - 7 =$ _____
50. $-2 + 5 =$ _____
51. $(-2)(-5) =$ _____
52. $-7 - 10 =$ _____
53. $-4(-10) =$ _____
54. $11 - 7 =$ _____
55. $-4 - 12 =$ _____
56. $7 - 10 =$ _____
57. $(-3)(-4)(-6) =$ _____
58. $-14 - 20 =$ _____
59. $-3 + 8 =$ _____
60. $0 - 4 =$ _____

Names _____

Group Activity 2

Directions: Simplify.

1. $-14 - 20 =$ _____
2. $(-3)(-4)(-3) =$ _____
3. $7 - 10 =$ _____
4. $-4 - 12 =$ _____
5. $11 - 7 =$ _____
6. $4(-10) =$ _____
7. $-7 - 10 =$ _____
8. $(-2)(-5) =$ _____
9. $-2 + 5 =$ _____
10. $-4 - 7 =$ _____
11. $-6 + 3 =$ _____
12. $-2 - 3 =$ _____
13. $-4 + 6 =$ _____
14. $-6(-3) =$ _____
15. $5 - 10 =$ _____
16. $10 - 4 =$ _____
17. $-2 - 6 =$ _____
18. $13 - 17 =$ _____
19. $-28 \div 7 =$ _____
20. $\frac{24}{-3} =$ _____
21. $0 \div 5 =$ _____
22. $\frac{7}{0} =$ _____
23. $-3 + 6 =$ _____
24. $7 - 9 =$ _____
25. $-3 - 6 =$ _____
26. $-3(6) =$ _____
27. $-7(-8) =$ _____
28. $5 - 9 =$ _____
29. $-6 - 10 =$ _____
30. $-3(-7) =$ _____
31. $-4 + 10 =$ _____
32. $-4 - 8 =$ _____
33. $-6 \div 2 =$ _____
34. $-32 \div -8 =$ _____
35. $16 - 20 =$ _____
36. $-5 - 6 =$ _____
37. $-1 - 1 =$ _____
38. $0 - 7 =$ _____
39. $(-3)(-2)(-1) =$ _____
40. $-3(7) + 5 =$ _____
41. $\frac{1}{2} \div \frac{-3}{5} =$ _____
42. $\frac{-6}{7} \div \frac{-3}{5} =$ _____
43. $\frac{-2}{3} \cdot \frac{3}{5} =$ _____
44. $-7(-4) - 20 =$ _____
45. $\frac{-6}{2} \div \frac{-12}{8} =$ _____
46. $\frac{-7 - 8}{-4 + 3} =$ _____
47. $-3 - 4 =$ _____
48. $-2(-7) =$ _____
49. $6 - 13 =$ _____
50. $6 - 2 =$ _____
51. $\frac{-30}{-6} =$ _____
52. $-8 - 3 =$ _____
53. $-7(6)(-3) =$ _____
54. $\frac{108}{-12} =$ _____
55. $10(4) + 6(-2) =$ _____
56. $-8 \div (-2) + 8 - 11 =$ _____
57. $-7(-3) - 24 =$ _____
58. $-6 - 20 =$ _____
59. $-3 + 8 =$ _____
60. $7 - 14 =$ _____

Name _____

Collecting Like Terms

Directions: Simplify.

1. $-3x + 4x - 6x =$ _____

2. $-3m - 3m =$ _____

3. $-6x + 5k - 4x - k =$ _____

4. $-3p + 4m - 4m - 6p =$ _____

5. $-8 + 5m - 6m =$ _____

6. $3p - 6a - 6a - 6p =$ _____

7. $-8x + 4y - 6x - 4y =$ _____

8. $-a - a =$ _____

9. $-4x^2 - 4x^2 + 8y - 10y =$ _____

10. $-x + 4y + 3y - 7x =$ _____

11. $-3m + 4m - 3m =$ _____

12. $-2x - 2x + 4y - 4y =$ _____

13. $-3p - 8p + 4x - p =$ _____

14. $6k + k - 3k =$ _____

15. $-8mn + 4mn - 3p - 2p =$ _____

16. $-2xy + 4x - 6y - 3xy =$ _____

17. $-2mn + 8mn - 6x - 3x =$ _____

18. $-3x + x =$ _____

19. $p + p =$ _____

20. $-6y - 6y =$ _____

Teacher Created Materials
PUBLISHING

#10623—Active Algebra—Algebra I, Guided Practice Book

Name _____

Distributing and Collecting

Directions: Simplify.

1. $7(x + 2) - 4$

2. $-3(m - 4) - 2m$

3. $-2(3k + 2) - 6k$

4. $7 + 3(2x - 6) - 3x$

5. $-2(2p - 4) - 6p - 3$

6. $-5(3n - 7) + 2n$

7. $-3(2x - 7) - 2x + 6$

8. $-6a - 4(2a + 7) - 7a$

9. $3x - (2x - 4) - 6x$

10. $3(4p - 7) - (2p + 3)$

11. $6m - (2m + 5) - 4m$

12. $3 - 4(6m + 1) - 5m$

13. $-4(2x - 7) - (3x - 7)$

14. $3 - 5(2p + 7) - 8p + 2$

15. $-(3x + 9) + 6x - x$

16. $2x - 7 - 3(5x + 6)$

17. $-7k - 3(2k + 3) - 2k$

18. $3(5m - 1) - 7m$

Teacher Created Materials
PUBLISHING

Name _____

Writing Equations Packet

Directions: Assign the variable and write an equation for each of the following. **Do not solve.**

1. The first of two numbers is 3 times the second. Their sum is 88. Find the numbers.

    Let _____ = _____

    _____ = _____

    Equation: _____

2. The length of a rectangular field is 10 meters less than 9 times the width. The perimeter is 140 meters. Find the length.

    Let _____ = _____

    _____ = _____

    Equation: _____

3. The larger of two numbers is 10 less than 5 times the smaller. Their sum is 146. Find the smaller number.

    Let _____ = _____

    _____ = _____

    Equation: _____

4. The perimeter of a rectangle is 482 cm. The length is 6 cm greater than 4 times the width. Find the length.

    Let _____ = _____

    _____ = _____

    Equation: _____

5. Together, a football and a basketball cost $65. A football costs $5 more than $\frac{1}{2}$ of what a basketball costs. How much does a football cost?

    Let _____ = _____

    _____ = _____

    Equation: _____

Writing Equations Packet *(cont.)*

6. The sum of three numbers is 75. The second number is 5 more than
    4 times the first, and the third is 2 times the first. Find the second number.

    Let _____ = _____

    _____ = _____

    _____ = _____

    Equation: _____

7. If 7 less than 4 times a number is 29, find the number.

    Let _____ = _____

    Equation: _____

8. Jan and Jill made $58 babysitting. Jan made $6 more than 3 times
    as much money as Jill made. How much money did Jan make?

    Let _____ = _____

    _____ = _____

    Equation: _____

9. José and Juan went running. José ran 2 miles less than $\frac{1}{2}$ as many miles
    as Juan. José ran 6 miles. How many miles did Juan run?

    Let _____ = _____

    _____ = _____

    Equation: _____

10. Together, a dresser, a nightstand, and a vanity cost $1,605. The dresser
    costs 3 times as much as the nightstand, and the vanity costs $300 more
    than the nightstand. Find the cost of the vanity.

    Let _____ = _____

    _____ = _____

    _____ = _____

    Equation: _____

Writing Equations Packet *(cont.)*

11. Mrs. Edgar cut a piece of wire that was 125 cm long into two pieces. The first piece was 10 cm less than 4 times the second. Find the length of both pieces of wire.

    Let _____ = _____

    _____ = _____

    Equation: _____

12. Chester, the dog, loves to eat treats. He has eaten twice as many today as yesterday. He has eaten a total of 15 dog treats in both days. How many treats has he eaten today?

    Let _____ = _____

    _____ = _____

    Equation: _____

13. The price for 2 student tickets and 4 adult tickets to a play is $50. Adult tickets are $5 more than student tickets. How much does each ticket cost?

    Let _____ = _____

    _____ = _____

    Equation: _____

14. The sum of two numbers is 73. One number is 3 greater than the other number. Find each number.

    Let _____ = _____

    _____ = _____

    Equation: _____

15. Together, a pair of shorts, jeans, and a T-shirt cost $37. The shorts cost $2 more than the jeans, and the shirt costs $3 less than the shorts. Find the cost of the shorts.

    Let _____ = _____

    _____ = _____

    _____ = _____

    Equation: _____

Writing Equations Packet (cont.)

16. Jasper High School has 47 drill team members. This is 18 less than 5 times the number of twirlers in the school. How many twirlers does the school have?

Let _____ = _____

_____ = _____

Equation: _____

17. A rectangle has a length that is 4 meters more than the width. The perimeter is 184 meters. Find the length.

Let _____ = _____

_____ = _____

Equation: _____

18. Bob bought one twin pack of video games for $42. This is $6 less than $\frac{2}{3}$ the cost of a triple pack of video games. What is the price of a triple pack of video games?

Let _____ = _____

_____ = _____

Equation: _____

19. Maria is 240 cm tall. This is 3 cm less than 3 times her height at birth. Find her height at birth.

Let _____ = _____

_____ = _____

Equation: _____

20. The electric guitar is $600 more than the acoustic guitar. The total cost of 1 acoustic and 1 electric guitar is $3,200. Find the price of an electric guitar.

Let _____ = _____

_____ = _____

Equation: _____

Writing Equations Packet (cont.)

21. Jawan's bike weighs 8 pounds more than Natasha's bike. Together, they weigh 100 pounds. Find the weight of Jawan's bike.

    Let _____ = _____

    _____ = _____

    Equation: _____

22. At the fair, Jack and Mike played a game of throwing darts at balloons. Jack popped 4 more balloons than Mike did. Together, they popped 8 balloons. How many balloons did Jack pop?

    Let _____ = _____

    _____ = _____

    Equation: _____

23. Jamal earned $4 more than 6 times what Dusty earned. Together, they earned $53. How much money did Jamal earn?

    Let _____ = _____

    _____ = _____

    Equation: _____

24. Judy worked 8 hours more than 6 times the number of hours Jake worked. Shamika worked 2 hours less than Judy worked. Shamika worked 30 hours. How many hours did Judy work?

    Let _____ = _____

    _____ = _____

    _____ = _____

    Equation: _____

25. A boom box costs $10 more than half the price of a CD player. How much is the CD player if the boom box costs $60?

    Let _____ = _____

    _____ = _____

    Equation: _____

Writing Equations Packet (cont.)

26. Lacey has 6 more than 7 times the number of marbles Rasheed has. Together, Lacey and Rasheed have 70 marbles. How many marbles does Lacey have?

    Let _____ = _____

    _____ = _____

    Equation: _____

27. Julio made $83 less than 7 times what Bo made. The sum of their earnings is $381. How much money did Bo make?

    Let _____ = _____

    _____ = _____

    Equation: _____

28. The number of CDs that CeDaniel owns is 6 less than 6 times the number of CDs that Charlie owns. Altogether, they own 78 CDs. How many CDs does CeDaniel own?

    Let _____ = _____

    _____ = _____

    Equation: _____

29. Kwan and Michael went on a 16-mile bike ride. Kwan finished in 60 minutes. Kwan finished 2 minutes less than $\frac{1}{5}$ of Michael's time. Find Michael's time.

    Let _____ = _____

    _____ = _____

    Equation: _____

30. Damon and Ryan ran 14 miles. Ryan ran 2 miles more than 3 times the distance Damon ran. How many miles did each boy run?

    Let _____ = _____

    _____ = _____

    Equation: _____

Writing Equations Packet (cont.)

31. Heather and Jeong Kim attended school a total of 183 days. Heather attended 9 days less than $\frac{1}{2}$ the days Jeong Kim attended. How many days did Heather attend school?

    Let _____ = _____

    _____ = _____

    Equation: _____

32. There are 90 rare birds from South Africa at the Houston Zoo. This is 3 times as many as the number of rare birds from Tanzania. How many Tanzanian rare birds are there at the Houston Zoo?

    Let _____ = _____

    _____ = _____

    Equation: _____

33. If you add $\frac{3}{4}$ of a number back to the number itself, you get 49. Find the number.

    Let _____ = _____

    Equation: _____

34. Darnell has 26 farm animals. The number of cows is 5 more than twice the number of horses. How many of each animal does he have?

    Let _____ = _____

    _____ = _____

    Equation: _____

35. Josh ran 2 miles more than $\frac{3}{8}$ the distance T.J. ran. Josh ran 5 miles. How many miles did T.J. run?

    Let _____ = _____

    _____ = _____

    Equation: _____

Writing Equations Packet *(cont.)*

36. Laron bowled two games. His first score was $\frac{1}{2}$ of his second score. He scored 330 points in the two games combined. How many points did he score in each game?

    Let _____ = _____

    _____ = _____

    Equation: _____

37. Joe, Tashika, and Damon went to the candy store. Together, they purchased a case of Super Sticky Candy. Damon pitched in $5 more than Tashika, and Joe pitched in twice the money Damon did. The case of candy costs $27. How much money did Joe pitch in for the candy?

    Let _____ = _____

    _____ = _____

    _____ = _____

    Equation: _____

38. Together, a bracelet and a ring cost $200. Find the price of each item if the bracelet costs 3 times as much as the ring.

    Let _____ = _____

    _____ = _____

    Equation: _____

39. LaRhonda and Nikki went to the mall. LaRhonda brought $\frac{2}{3}$ the amount of money that Nikki brought. LaRhonda brought $80. How much money did Nikki bring to the mall?

    Let _____ = _____

    _____ = _____

    Equation: _____

40. There were a total of 72 geese in two flocks. One flock was 3 times greater than the other. How many geese were in each flock?

    Let _____ = _____

    _____ = _____

    Equation: _____

Writing Equations Packet (cont.)

41. Stephanie and Ming Lee earned a total of $52 for mowing lawns this summer. Ming Lee earned $10 more than $\frac{1}{5}$ of what Stephanie earned. How much money did Ming Lee earn?

    Let _____ = _____

    _____ = _____

    Equation: _____

42. The perimeter of a triangle is 44 meters. Side one is 8 meters longer than side two, and side three is twice as long as side one. Find the length of each side.

    Let _____ = _____

    _____ = _____

    _____ = _____

    Equation: _____

43. The perimeter of a rectangle is 42 cm. The width is 7 cm less than the length. Find the dimensions of the rectangle.

    Let _____ = _____

    _____ = _____

    Equation: _____

44. Last week, Tracy and Julio walked 17 miles together. Julio walked 1 mile less than 2 times the distance Tracy walked. How many miles did each boy walk?

    Let _____ = _____

    _____ = _____

    Equation: _____

45. Jamie spent $7.61 at the convenience store. This is $3.50 more than 3 times the amount of money that Erin spent. How much money did Erin spend?

    Let _____ = _____

    _____ = _____

    Equation: _____

Writing Equations Packet (cont.)

46. Kerry, Lexy, and Lacy went to a popular clothing store and spent a total of $500.00. Lacy spent $5 more than $\frac{1}{2}$ of what Lexy spent, and Kerry spent three times what Lacy spent. Find the amount of money each girl spent.

    Let _____ = _____

    _____ = _____

    _____ = _____

    Equation: _____

47. There are 20 apples and oranges in the grocery store. There are 6 more apples than oranges. How many apples are in the store?

    Let _____ = _____

    _____ = _____

    Equation: _____

48. Oriana spent $16 at the concession stand. This is $4 less than twice what her friend Amber spent. How much money did Amber spend at the concession stand?

    Let _____ = _____

    _____ = _____

    Equation: _____

Names _____

Cups and Chips 1

Directions: Solve the following equations, using cups and chips.

1. $2x - 3 = 5x - 1$

2. $4x + 2 = -2x - 3$

3. $3x - 2 = -5x + 2$

4. $4x + 2 = 2x - 1$

5. $6x - 3 = 4x + 1$

6. $-2x + 3 = x - 2$

Names _____

Cups and Chips 2

Directions: Solve the following equations, using cups and chips.

1. $2x + 3 = x + 1$

2. $-3x + 5 = 2x - 1$

3. $x - 2 = 3x + 1$

4. $3x - 3 = 4 + 2x - 6$

5. $-1x + 5 = 2x - 2$

6. $-2x + 1x - 5 = 3x + 2$

Names _____

Cups and Chips 3

Directions: Solve the following equations, using cups and chips.

1. $2x - 3 = 1x + 4$

2. $3x - 2 = 2x - 4$

3. $3x - 6x - 2 = 2x - x + 3$

4. $-2x = -3x + 5x - 3$

5. $4x - 2 = 2x + 5$

6. $-4x - 2x - 3 = 2x - 5$

Name _____

Solving Equations 1

Directions: Solve. Show all work.

1. $2x + 3 = 6x - 5$

2. $8x + 4 = 6x - 1$

3. $4x - 2 = 6x + 3$

4. $8m - 4 = 3m + 8$

5. $4p - 3 = 8p + 5$

6. $8k + 4 = 2k - 3$

7. $3x - 5x + 4 = 6x - 2 - 3x$

8. $2p + 3 - 5 = 6p - 8 - 10p$

9. $8 - 4m - 6m = 3m - 4m + 2$

10. $3k + 1 - 6k = 4k + 8 - 9k$

11. $6x - 5 = 3x + 1$

12. $4x - 7 = 2x$

Name _____

Solving Equations 2

Directions: Solve. Show all work.

1. $3x - 4 = 7x + 2$ **2.** $6p + 2 = -3p + 1$ **3.** $4m - 7 = 8m + 2$

4. $5x + 1 = 7x - 3$ **5.** $2m - 3 = 6m - 4$ **6.** $8a + 3 = 6a + 2$

7. $3x + 2x - 1 = 7x - 5 - 5$ **8.** $3a - 5a - 2 = 6a + a - 7$

9. $2x - 3 = 7x + 3 - 4x$ **10.** $4x + 5 = 10x - 6$

  Teacher Created Materials
PUBLISHING

Solving Equations 2 (cont.)

11. $5f + 2 - 4 = 2f - 4f - 8$

12. $-8x - 6 = -9x - 4$

13. $7a + 9 - a = 3a + 4$

14. $10x + 6 = 7x + 5 + 1$

15. $-x - 2 = 4x + 6$

16. $3z + 12 = 6z + 10$

17. $6y - 8 - y = 19 + 9y$

18. $8x + 1 = 2x + 3$

19. $-9u - 17 = -5u - 7$

20. $11n - (-6) = 13n - 3$

Name _____

Adding and Subtracting Fractions

Directions: Calculate.

1. $-3 - 1\dfrac{1}{3}$

2. $6 + 2\dfrac{1}{2}$

3. $-4 - 2\dfrac{3}{5}$

4. $8 - 3\dfrac{2}{3}$

5. $-6\dfrac{1}{2} - 3\dfrac{1}{4}$

6. $5\dfrac{1}{4} - 3\dfrac{2}{5}$

7. $-4\dfrac{3}{4} + 6\dfrac{1}{3}$

8. $-7\dfrac{1}{8} - 4\dfrac{1}{2}$

9. $6\dfrac{2}{5} - 3\dfrac{1}{3}$

10. $-6 - 4\dfrac{2}{3}$

11. $-8 + 2\dfrac{1}{2}$

12. $-10 + 4\dfrac{1}{5}$

Name _____

Multiplying and Dividing Fractions

Directions: Calculate.

1. $-3 \cdot 2\frac{1}{3}$

2. $6 \div -1\frac{1}{2}$

3. $-4 \cdot -5\frac{2}{5}$

4. $-3\frac{3}{4} \div 2$

5. $-5\frac{1}{2} \div -3$

6. $-4\frac{3}{4} \cdot 7$

7. $-6\frac{2}{3} \div -3$

8. $-4 \cdot -2\frac{3}{4}$

9. $-6 \div 2\frac{1}{3}$

10. $8\frac{1}{2} \div -2$

11. $-10\frac{2}{3} \div -3$

12. $-4 \cdot -6\frac{1}{4}$

Name _____

Algebra Applications with Angles

Directions: Solve for the variable and find the measure of each angle.

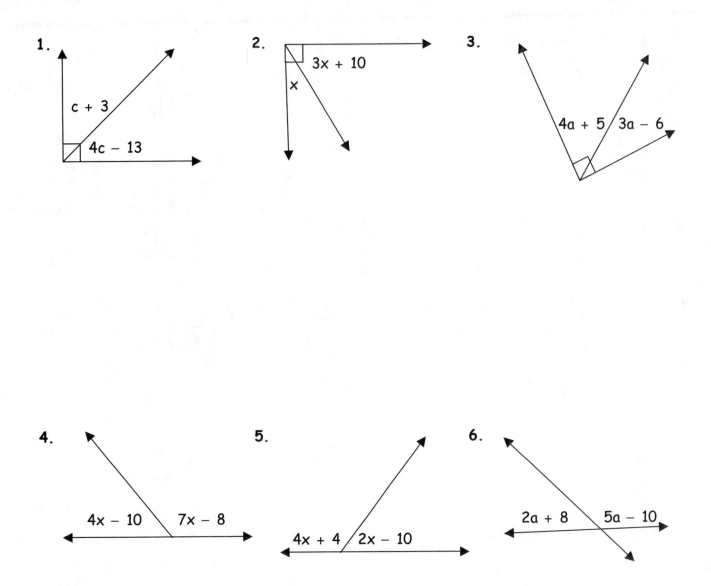

1.

$c + 3$

$4c - 13$

2.

$3x + 10$

x

3.

$4a + 5$ $3a - 6$

4.

$4x - 10$ $7x - 8$

5.

$4x + 4$ $2x - 10$

6.

$2a + 8$ $5a - 10$

Teacher Created Materials
PUBLISHING

Algebra Applications with Angles (cont.)

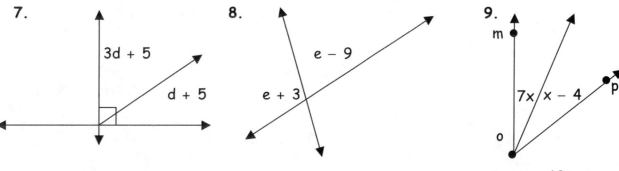

7.
3d + 5
d + 5

8.
e − 9
e + 3

9.
m
7x / x − 4
o
p
∠mop = 60°

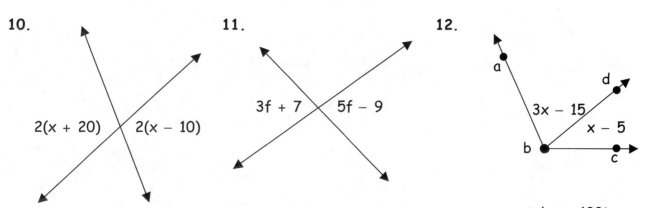

10.
2(x + 20)   2(x − 10)

11.
3f + 7   5f − 9

12.
a
d
3x − 15
x − 5
b
c
∠abc = 100°

Name _____

Mixed Fractions

Directions: Calculate.

1. $-3 \cdot 2\frac{1}{2}$

2. $-3 - 1\frac{1}{3}$

3. $-6 \div 1\frac{1}{2}$

4. $6 + 2\frac{1}{2}$

5. $-4 \cdot 5\frac{2}{5}$

6. $-4 - 2\frac{3}{5}$

7. $-3\frac{3}{4} \div 2$

8. $-8 + 3\frac{2}{3}$

9. $5\frac{1}{2} \div -3$

Mixed Fractions (cont.)

10. $6\dfrac{1}{2} - 3\dfrac{1}{4}$

11. $-4\dfrac{3}{4} \cdot 7$

12. $-5\dfrac{1}{4} - 3\dfrac{2}{5}$

13. $-6\dfrac{2}{3} \div 3$

14. $-4\dfrac{3}{4} + 6\dfrac{1}{3}$

15. $-4 \cdot 2\dfrac{3}{4}$

16. $-8\dfrac{1}{2} \div 2$

17. $-7\dfrac{1}{8} - 4\dfrac{1}{2}$

18. $-10\dfrac{2}{3} \div -3$

Name _____

Literal Equations 1

Directions: Solve each of the following equations for the specified variable.

1. $P = 2l + 2w$, for w _____

2. $A = \dfrac{1}{2}(b_1 + b_2)h$, for b_1 _____

3. $V = \dfrac{1}{3}Bh$, for h _____

4. $A = \dfrac{1}{2}bh$, for b _____

5. $C = 2\pi r$, for π _____

6. $I = prt$, for t _____

7. $\tan x = \dfrac{o}{a}$, for a _____

8. $a^2 + b^2 = c^2$, for a _____

9. $A = \dfrac{1}{2}(b_1 + b_2)h$, for b_2 _____

10. $A = lw$, for w _____

11. $A = \pi r^2$, for π _____

12. $\sin x = \dfrac{o}{h}$, for h _____

13. $C = \pi d$, for d _____

14. $d = rt$, for t _____

15. $C = \pi d$, for π _____

16. $a^2 + b^2 = c^2$, for b _____

17. $V = \dfrac{1}{3}Bh$, for B _____

18. $V = \pi r^2 h$, for r _____

Name _____

Literal Equations 2

Directions: Solve each of the following equations for the specified variable.

1. $A = lw$, for l _____

2. $P = 2l + 2w$, for w _____

3. $A = \frac{1}{2}(b_1 + b_2)h$, for h _____

4. $A = \frac{1}{2}bh$, for h _____

5. $\tan x = \frac{o}{a}$, for a _____

6. $I = prt$, for r _____

7. $A = \frac{1}{2}bh$, for b _____

8. $A = lw$, for w _____

9. $a^2 + b^2 = c^2$, for b _____

10. $A = \frac{1}{2}(b_1 + b_2)h$, for b_1 _____

11. $C = 2\pi r$, for r _____

12. $\tan x = \frac{o}{a}$, for o _____

13. $A = bh$, for b _____

14. $\sin x = \frac{o}{h}$, for h _____

15. $A = \frac{1}{2}(b_1 + b_2)h$, for b_2 _____

16. $A = bh$, for h _____

17. $a^2 + b^2 = c^2$, for a _____

18. $V = \pi r^2 h$, for r _____

Name _____

Writing Equations Review

Directions: Write equations to satisfy the following. **Do not solve.**

1. Let x = Beth's age
    2x + 3 = John's age
    4x − 6 = Ashley's age

    A. The sum of Beth and Ashley's ages is 84. _____

    B. John and Beth are the same age. _____

    C. John's age is 12. _____

    D. The sum of all three ages is 120. _____

2. Let x = cost of hamburger
    x + $.20 = cost of cheeseburger
    3x − $1.10 = cost of double-meat cheeseburger

    A. Total cost of a hamburger and a cheeseburger is $3.50. _____

    B. The cost of 2 cheeseburgers is the same as 1 double-meat cheeseburger.

    _____

    C. Altogether, 3 hamburgers and a cheeseburger cost the same as 2 double-meat

    cheeseburgers.

    _____

3. Let x = cost of a CD
    x − 3 = cost of a tape
    3x − 1 = cost of a DVD movie

    A. A CD and a tape cost $20. _____

    B. The cost of 5 CDs is the same as 2 DVD movies. _____

    C. A DVD movie costs $20. _____

4. Let w = width
    2w − 1 = length

    A. The length is 240 cm. _____

    B. The perimeter of the rectangle is 600 cm. _____

    C. The area of the rectangle is 2,400 sq cm. _____

Writing Equations Review *(cont.)*

5.   Let x = 1st number
2x − 5 = 2nd number
4x + 10 = 3rd number

A. The second number is 20. _____

B. The sum of the first two numbers is equal to the third number.

_____

C. The second number doubled is equal to 4 times the first number.

_____

6.   Let x = cost of a motorcycle
50x + 5,000 = cost of a truck
30x − 1,000 = cost of a car

A. The total cost of 1 car, 1 truck, and 1 motorcycle is $47,000.

_____

B. The cost of 3 motorcycles and 2 cars is the same as 2 trucks. _____

C. The cost of a truck is $25,000. _____

7.   Let x = cost of 1 pair of sandals
2x − 30 = cost of 1 pair of tennis shoes
3x − 70 = cost of 1 pair of boots

A. The cost of 1 pair of boots is $80. _____

B. Altogether, 1 pair of sandals and 1 pair of boots cost $130.

_____

C. The tennis shoes cost the same as the boots. _____

D. The cost of 3 pairs of sandals and 1 pair of tennis shoes is the same as 2 pairs of boots and 1 pair of sandals. _____

Writing Equations Review *(cont.)*

8. Let L = length

    $\frac{1}{2}$L − 2 = width

    A. The width is 25 meters._____

    B. The perimeter of the rectangle is 200 meters. _____

    C. The area of the rectangle is 1,875 meters. _____

    D. Exactly 4 times the width equals twice the length. _____

9. Let x = cost of science book

    2x − 3 = cost of math book

    4x − 1 = cost of English book

    A. The cost of 1 math book is $24. _____

    B. The cost of 1 English book is $28. _____

    C. Altogether, 2 math books cost the same as 3 science books. _____

10. Let x = cost of shirt

    3x − 2 = cost of jeans

    5x − 15 = cost of shoes

    A. The jeans cost $55. _____

    B. The shoes cost $55. _____

    C. The jeans cost the same as the shoes. _____

    D. The shirt, jeans, and shoes cost $138 altogether.

    _____

11. Let w = width

    4w − 2 = length

    A. The length is 22 cm. _____

    B. The perimeter of the rectangle is 56 cm. _____

    C. The area of the rectangle is 400 cm^2. _____

Writing Equations Review *(cont.)*

12. Let x = number of small drinks sold

    $3x - 4$ = number of medium drinks sold

    $7x + 4$ = number of large drinks sold

    A. 35 medium drinks were sold. _____

    B. 95 large drinks were sold. _____

    C. Exactly 3 times the number of large drinks is the same as 6 times the number

    of small drinks. _____

    D. Altogether, 143 drinks were sold. _____

13. Let x = larger number

    $\frac{1}{2}x - 2$ = smaller number

    A. The smaller number is 22. _____

    B. Altogether, their sum is 22. _____

    C. If you triple the smaller number, and double the larger number, their sum is 206.

    _____

    D. Exactly 5 times the smaller number is the same as 2 times the larger number.

    _____

Name _____

Literal Equations 3

Directions: Solve each of the following equations for the specified variable.

1. $a^2 + b^2 = c^2$, for c _____

2. $A = bh$, for b _____

3. $\tan x = \dfrac{o}{a}$, for a _____

4. $A = \pi r^2$, for r _____

5. $V = \dfrac{1}{3}Bh$, for B _____

6. $C = \pi d$, for d _____

7. $S = 2\pi rh$, for h _____

8. $A = \dfrac{bh}{2}$, for b _____

9. $a^2 + b^2 = c^2$, for b _____

10. $V = \dfrac{1}{3}bh$, for h _____

11. $P = 2(l + w)$, for w _____

12. $C = \pi d$, for d _____

13. $d = rt$, for t _____

14. $A = \dfrac{1}{2}(b_1 + b_2)h$, for b_2 _____

15. $\sin x = \dfrac{o}{h}$, for o _____

16. $a^2 + b^2 = c^2$, for a _____

17. $P = 2l + 2w$, for l _____

18. $C = 2\pi r$, for π _____

Teacher Created Materials
PUBLISHING

#10623—Active Algebra—Algebra I, Guided Practice Book

Name _____

Percent of Region Packet

Directions: Shade the given percent of each region.

1. 50%

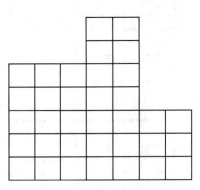

Number of blocks shaded:_____

2. 25%

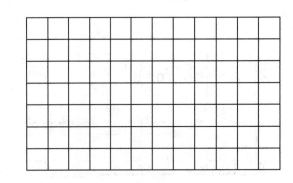

Number of blocks shaded:_____

3. 60%

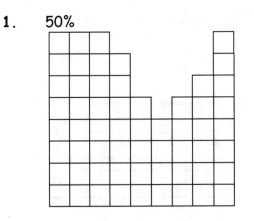

Number of blocks shaded:_____

4. 12.5%

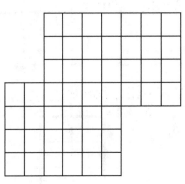

Number of blocks shaded:_____

5. 87.5%

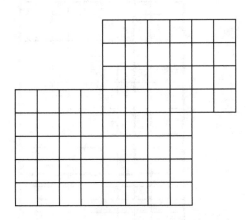

Number of blocks shaded:_____

6. 30%

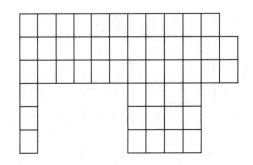

Number of blocks shaded:_____

Teacher Created Materials
PUBLISHING

Percent of Region Packet (cont.)

Directions: Count the number of squares in each region and complete the answer sheet.

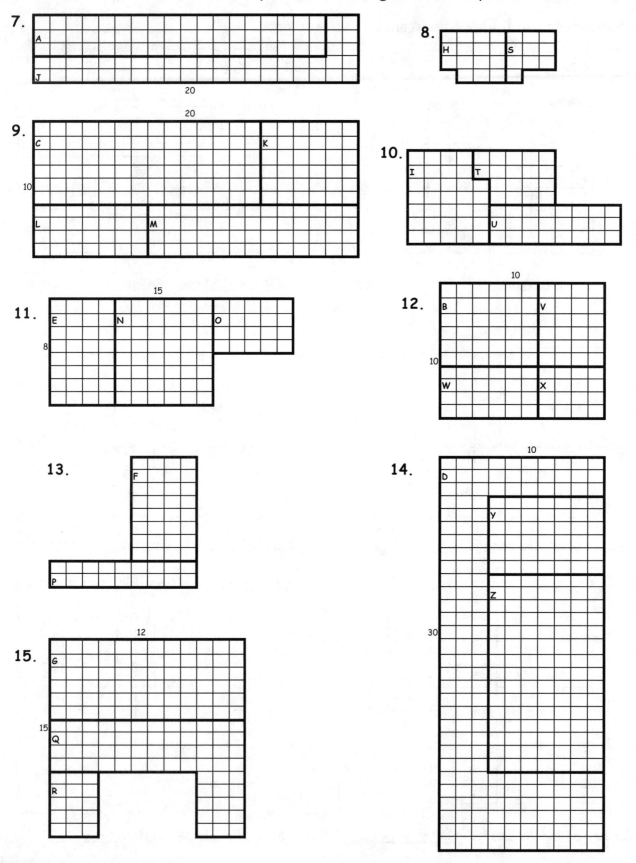

Percent of Region Packet (cont.)

Directions: Record your answers on this chart.

		# of Boxes	Fraction	Decimal	Percent
7.	A				%
	J				%
	Total				%
8.	H				%
	S				%
	Total				%
9.	C				%
	K				%
	L				%
	M				%
	Total				%
10.	I				%
	T				%
	U				%
	Total				%
11.	E				%
	N				%
	O				%
	Total				%

Teacher Created Materials
PUBLISHING

Percent of Region Packet (cont.)

Directions: Record your answers on this chart.

		# of Boxes	Fraction	Decimal	Percent
12.	B				%
	V				%
	W				%
	X				%
	Total				%
13.	F				%
	P				%
	Total				%
14.	D				%
	Y				%
	Z				%
	Total				%
15.	G				%
	Q				%
	R				%
	Total				%

Name _____

Percent of Region Notes

Directions: Shade the given percent of each region.

1. 87.5%

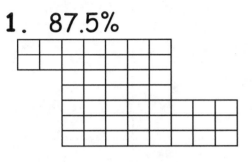

2. 20%

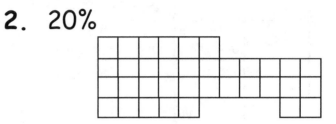

Number of boxes shaded:_____

Number of boxes shaded:_____

Directions: Count the number of squares in each region and complete the answer sheet.

3.

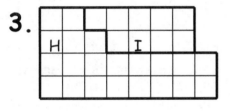

4.

		# of Boxes	Fraction	Decimal	Percent
3.	H				%
	I				%
	Total		▓▓▓▓	▓▓▓▓	%
4.	I				%
	T				%
	U				%
	Total		▓▓▓▓	▓▓▓▓	%

Teacher Created Materials
PUBLISHING

Name _____

Percent 1

Directions: Set up each proportion and solve. Write a "therefore statement" for each solution.

1.   The Riddicks insured their house for 80% of its value. If the house is valued at $74,000, how much is it insured for?

Proportion   Solve

2.   The Maddings insured their house for $70,000, which is 70% of its value. What is the value of their house?

Proportion   Solve

3.   The Smiths insured their house for 85% of its value. If the house is valued at $115,200, how much is it insured for?

Proportion   Solve

4.   Jamar scored 80% on a test and got 20 problems correct. How many problems were on the test?

Proportion   Solve

5.   Brittany scored 84% on a test and got 8 problems wrong. How many problems were on the test?

Proportion   Solve

6.   Raul scored 72% on a test and got 7 problems wrong. How many problems were on the test?

Proportion   Solve

Teacher Created Materials
PUBLISHING

#10623—Active Algebra—Algebra I, Guided Practice Book

Percent 1 (cont.)

7. Rose received a commission of 5% on the sale of a new house. If the selling price of the house was $61,000, what was Rose's commission?

   <u>Proportion</u>   <u>Solve</u>

8. Nicholas sold a new truck for $18,500 and made $1,295 in commission. What was his rate of commission?

   <u>Proportion</u>   <u>Solve</u>

9. On Wednesday, Just Deals received a shipment of 40 cases of cereal. This was 80% of the cases of cereal ordered. How many cases of cereal were ordered?

   <u>Proportion</u>   <u>Solve</u>

10. On Tuesday, Joshua Tree Nursery received a shipment of 80 peach trees. The manager had ordered 100 peach trees. What percent of trees were delivered?

    <u>Proportion</u>   <u>Solve</u>

11. Brandy made 60 out of 80 free throws that she attempted. What percent were successful throws?

    <u>Proportion</u>   <u>Solve</u>

12. Jonathon made 80% of his shots during the basketball season. If he made 140 shots, how many shots did he attempt?

    <u>Proportion</u>   <u>Solve</u>

Name _____

Probability

Directions: Solve these problems, and choose the best answer for each.

1. If 3 nickels are flipped at the same time, what is the probability that all 3 nickels will show tails?

   A. $\frac{3}{8}$ B. $\frac{1}{2}$ C. $\frac{1}{8}$ D. $\frac{1}{6}$

2. How many possible outcomes exist if a 6-sided die is rolled and then a spinner with 3 sections is spun?

   A. 9   B. 6   C. 3   D. 18

3. What is the probability of tossing a coin and getting tails, and then rolling a die and getting an odd number?

   A. $\frac{1}{3}$ B. $\frac{3}{4}$ C. $\frac{3}{8}$ D. $\frac{1}{4}$

4. A drawer contains 3 white pairs of socks, 2 black pairs of socks, and 4 brown pairs of socks. Without replacing the socks, what is the probability of choosing a black pair, a white pair, and then a brown pair?

   A. $\frac{1}{21}$ B. $\frac{8}{243}$ C. $\frac{1}{8}$ D. $\frac{1}{7}$

5. The Snack Shack has 4 different soda pops, 6 different types of chips, and 10 different types of candy. How many possible combinations exist?

   A. 20   B. 240   C. 180   D. 54

6. Jaron has 3 red shirts, 4 blue shirts, and 5 white shirts in his closet. If he picks 1 shirt without looking, what is the probability that it will be blue?

   A. $\frac{1}{3}$ B. $\frac{1}{4}$ C. $\frac{5}{12}$ D. $\frac{2}{5}$

7. In how many different ways can all 3 of the pictures be arranged in a row?

   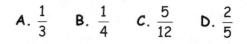

   A. 9   B. 3   C. 4   D. 6

8. A purse contains 2 silver dollars, 4 pennies, 2 nickels, 4 dimes, and 6 quarters. Without looking, what is the probability of picking a quarter, not putting it back, and then picking another quarter?

   A. $\frac{5}{51}$ B. $\frac{30}{256}$ C. $\frac{5}{31}$ D. $\frac{5}{8}$

9. Over a four-week period, Chang earned $52.25, $48.25, $51.25, and $50.25. What is his mean pay?

   A. $51   C. $50.50
   B. $49.50   D. $51.50

10. Jaden's grades in Algebra are 85, 92, 83, 85, 98, and 74. What is the mode?

    A. 86   B. 85   C. 87   D. 88

11. How many ways can 4 people stand in a line?

    A. 6   B. 8   C. 12   D. 24

Probability (cont.)

12. If each spinner is spun once, how many possible outcomes exist?

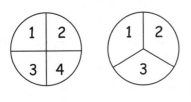

A. 7   B. 12   C. 8   D. 10

13. What is the probability of spinning a 4 on the first spinner and then spinning a 2 on the second spinner?

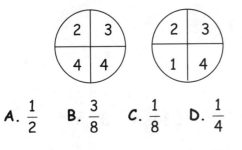

A. $\frac{1}{2}$ B. $\frac{3}{8}$ C. $\frac{1}{8}$ D. $\frac{1}{4}$

14. There are 10 girls and 14 boys in Mrs. Robin's Algebra I class. All of the students' names are in a bag. Without looking, what is the probability of choosing a girl's name?

A. $\frac{7}{12}$ B. $\frac{5}{12}$ C. $\frac{3}{5}$ D. $\frac{4}{7}$

15. If the digits cannot be repeated, how many 4-digit numbers can be formed by using the digits 4, 8, 1, 6, and 3?

A. 125   B. 40   C. 120   D. 625

16. If digits cannot be repeated, how many 3-digit numbers can be formed by using the digits 8, 4, 2, and 5?

A. 24   B. 64   C. 256   D. 625

17. How many different ways can all 5 of the cards be arranged in row?

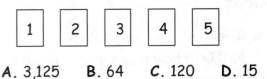

A. 3,125   B. 64   C. 120   D. 15

18. A police officer wrote speeding tickets to 5 different drivers. Their speeds were 72, 77, 75, 82, and 80. What was their mean speed?

A. 76.2   B. 78.2   C. 77.0   D. 77.2

19. Joaquin keeps all of his markers in a bag. He has 4 red markers, 6 blue markers, and 4 black markers. Without replacing the markers, what is the probability of drawing a black marker, a red marker, and then a blue marker?

A. $\frac{4}{9}$ B. $\frac{4}{91}$ C. $\frac{3}{51}$ D. $\frac{5}{51}$

20. Joshua listed his grades in history on a sheet of paper. His grades are 68, 75, 82, 92, 87, 82, and 88. What is his mean grade?

A. 65   B. 92   C. 75   D. 82

Name _____

Percent 2

Directions: Set up each proportion and solve. Write a "therefore statement" for each solution.

1. The Jacksons insured their house for 85% of its value. If the house is valued at $88,000 how much is it insured for?

    <u>Proportion</u>   <u>Solve</u>

2. Bridgette scored 90% on a test and got 4 problems wrong. How many problems were on the test?

    <u>Proportion</u>   <u>Solve</u>

3. A baseball glove was purchased at a discount of 30% for $84. What was the price of the glove before the discount?

    <u>Proportion</u>   <u>Solve</u>

4. The Houston Texans won 12 out of 16 football games. What percent did they lose?

    <u>Proportion</u>   <u>Solve</u>

5. Tayshawn bought a car stereo for $250. He had to make a down payment of $75. What percent did he pay as a down payment?

    <u>Proportion</u>   <u>Solve</u>

6. Gus received a commission of 6% on the sale of a pair of shoes. If the shoes cost $60, how much did he receive as a commission?

    <u>Proportion</u>   <u>Solve</u>

Percent 2 (cont.)

7. A logging company cut 72 trees on a piece of property. This was 90% of the trees on the property. How many trees were originally on the property?

    Proportion   Solve

8. Antwan got 84 hits out of 400 trips to the plate during the baseball season. What percent of his attempts were hits?

    Proportion   Solve

9. The Bulldogs won 24 out of 30 games this season. What percent of their games did they win?

    Proportion   Solve

10. Jordan bought a truck for $8,000 and paid 20% as a down payment. How much money did he give as a down payment?

    Proportion   Solve

11. The manager of Regal Shoes put a pair of shoes on sale for $48. The original cost of the shoes was $60. What percent was saved?

    Proportion   Solve

12. On Thursday, Juan spent 6 hours studying for his algebra exam. What percent of his day did he spend studying for the exam?

    Proportion   Solve

Name _____

Percents Review

Directions: Solve.

1. There are 85 members of the Key Club at Kennard High School. For a fundraiser, $\frac{7}{8}$ of them sold candy. To find the number of students who sold candy, multiply the number of students by _____.
   decimal

2. Exactly 50% of the freshman class went on a field trip. To find out how many of the 48 students went, multiply the number of students by _____.
   decimal

3. What is 60% as a decimal? _____   as a fraction? _____

4. What is $\frac{1}{8}$ as a decimal? _____   as a percent? _____

5. A shirt is on sale for $\frac{3}{5}$ off of the regular price of $10.

   A. Multiply the regular price by _____ to find the amount saved.
   decimal

   B. How much money was saved? _____

   C. How much money was spent? _____

   D. What percent is saved? _____

   E. What percent was spent? _____

6. Nicole scored 4 out of the 5 runs in the game. What percent did she score?
   <u>Proportion</u>   <u>Solve</u>

   What percent did she not score? _____

Percents Review *(cont.)*

7. Scott is going to spend 30% of his savings on new shoes. He has $150 saved.
   How much is he going to spend on the shoes?
   <u>Proportion</u>   <u>Solve</u>

8. If you shade 12 out of 16 blocks, what percent did you shade?
   <u>Proportion</u>   <u>Solve</u>

   What percent was not shaded? _____

9. If there are 40 problems on a test, how many need to be correct to make
   at least an 80%?
   <u>Proportion</u>   <u>Solve</u>

Name _____

Quick Percents

Directions: Solve.

1. What is the correct way to express $\frac{2}{5}$ as a percent? _____.

2. A pair of shoes that originally cost $24 is on a sale table marked "25% off." To find the amount of savings, multiply $24 by _____.
   decimal

3. A motorcycle is discounted 12.5% off of the original retail price of $8,495.25. To find the discounted amount, multiply the original price by _____.
   decimal

4. What is .3 expressed as a percent?
   _____%

5. The correct way to express $\frac{8}{20}$ as a decimal is _____.

6. What fraction of a dollar is $0.48?
   _____

7. Exactly 60% of the students at Central High School attended the school play. What fraction of the students attended the play?
   _____

8. The correct way to express 0.75 as a fraction is _____.

9. The correct way to express 0.7% as a decimal is _____.

10. In all, 80% of the 240 students passed the test. To find out how many students passed, multiply 240 by _____.
    fraction

11. A school survey indicates that $\frac{1}{5}$ of the people surveyed prefer orange juice to milk. 400 people took the survey. To find out how many people prefer orange juice, multiply the number of participants by _____.
    decimal

12. Which is the correct way to write 6% as a fraction? _____

13. Which is the correct way to write 0.685 as a percent? _____%

14. Amy entered a dance marathon. Of the 200 dancers who entered the contest, only $\frac{7}{8}$ of the dancers finished. To find how many of the dancers finished the contest, multiply 200 by _____.
    decimal

15. The correct way to write $\frac{4}{5}$ as a percent is _____%.

16. Altogether, $\frac{3}{8}$ of all shoppers bought the batteries that were on sale. What percent of shoppers bought batteries that were on sale?
    _____%

17. The correct way to write 0.25 as a percent is _____%.

Name _____

Proportions 1

Directions: Set up each proportion and solve. Show your work.

1. Julio gets 3 hits every 8 times at bat. At this same rate, how many hits will he get after 200 times at bat?

   Record and bubble your answer below.

2. Serena bought Christmas presents over the Internet last year. Before Christmas, 14 out of 16 items arrived. What percent of her order arrived before Christmas?

   Record and bubble your answer below.

3. A box of cake mix that makes one cake calls for $\frac{1}{4}$ cup of oil. Mia has $3\frac{1}{2}$ cups of oil. How many cakes can she make?

   Record and bubble your answer below.

Proportions 1 (cont.)

4. Mutt's Snack Store stocks 3 candy bars for every 7 bags of chips. If the manager counts an inventory of 45 candy bars, what is the total number of snacks in the store?

Record and bubble your answer below.

						.		
⊕ ⊖	⓪ ① ② ③ ④ ⑤ ⑥ ⑦ ⑧ ⑨	⓪ ① ② ③ ④ ⑤ ⑥ ⑦ ⑧ ⑨	⓪ ① ② ③ ④ ⑤ ⑥ ⑦ ⑧ ⑨	⓪ ① ② ③ ④ ⑤ ⑥ ⑦ ⑧ ⑨	⓪ ① ② ③ ④ ⑤ ⑥ ⑦ ⑧ ⑨		⓪ ① ② ③ ④ ⑤ ⑥ ⑦ ⑧ ⑨	⓪ ① ② ③ ④ ⑤ ⑥ ⑦ ⑧ ⑨

5. Lauren types 5 documents every 4 hours. At this rate, how many hours will it take her to type 300 documents?

   A.   200 hours
   B.   240 hours
   C.   375 hours
   D.   420 hours

6. Jerry's salary is $24,000 per year. How much money will Jerry earn in 9 months?

   A. $4,500
   B. $10,000
   C. $18,000
   D. $216,000

7. A map key shows that every 3 centimeters represents 50 miles. How many miles is represented by 12 centimeters?

   A.   .72 miles
   B.   6.25 miles
   C.   100 miles
   D.   200 miles

Proportions 1 (cont.)

8. Over the last three seasons, the PSJA North Raiders basketball team won 3 out of every 5 games. If they played 70 games, how many games did they lose?

    A. 28 games
    B. 42 games
    C. 175 games
    D. 200 games

9. Last Friday, 7 out of every 8 students enrolled in Algebra I at Mabank High School passed the unit test. If 200 students took the test, how many students failed?

    A. 40 students
    B. 200 students
    C. 175 students
    D. 25 students

10. The semester ratio of quizzes to test is 6:1. If there are 77 grades taken during the semester, how many are tests?

    A. 5 tests
    B. 7 tests
    C. 11 tests
    D. 14 tests

11. This year, 231 boys signed up to play baseball. Altogether, 6 out of every 7 boys sold candy for the league. How many boys chose not to sell candy?

    A. 27 boys
    B. 33 boys
    C. 35 boys
    D. 42 boys

Name _____

Measurement Review

Directions: Find the formula(s) for each of the following.

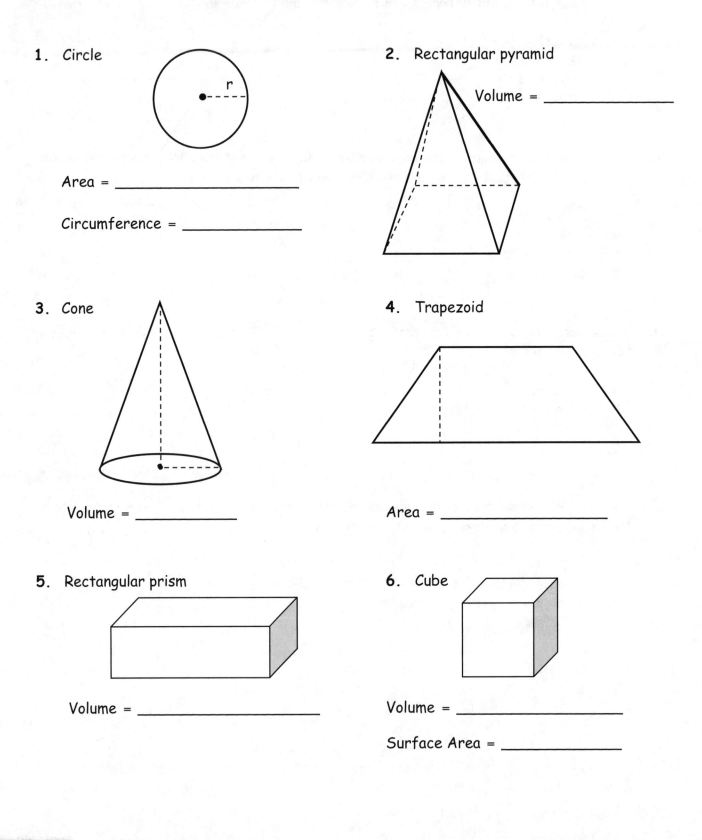

1. Circle

   Area = _____

   Circumference = _____

2. Rectangular pyramid

   Volume = _____

3. Cone

   Volume = _____

4. Trapezoid

   Area = _____

5. Rectangular prism

   Volume = _____

6. Cube

   Volume = _____

   Surface Area = _____

Measurement Review (cont.)

7. Find the area or volume of the following shapes with the given dimensions.

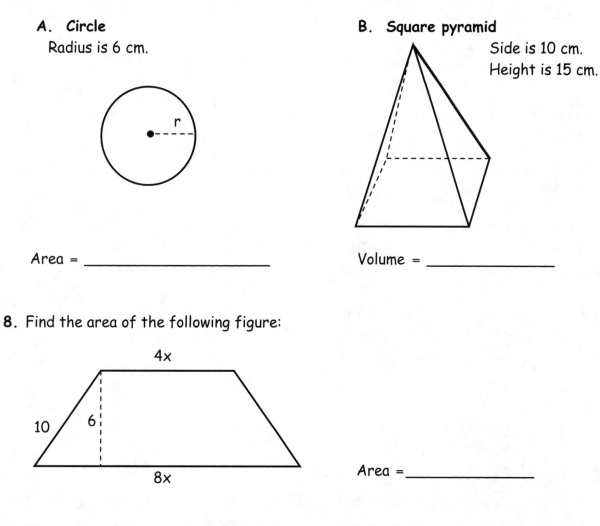

A. Circle

Radius is 6 cm.

Area = _____

B. Square pyramid

Side is 10 cm.
Height is 15 cm.

Volume = _____

8. Find the area of the following figure:

4x

10

6

8x

Area =_____

9. Which formula can be used to find the volume of the following composite solid?

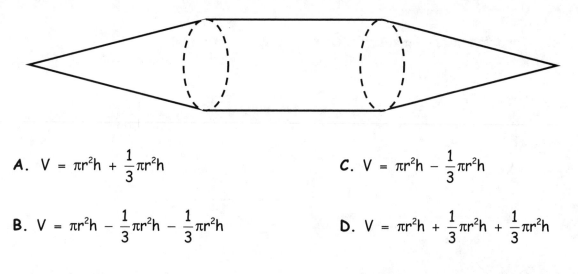

A. $V = \pi r^2 h + \frac{1}{3}\pi r^2 h$

C. $V = \pi r^2 h - \frac{1}{3}\pi r^2 h$

B. $V = \pi r^2 h - \frac{1}{3}\pi r^2 h - \frac{1}{3}\pi r^2 h$

D. $V = \pi r^2 h + \frac{1}{3}\pi r^2 h + \frac{1}{3}\pi r^2 h$

Measurement Review (cont.)

10. Find the surface area of the following net.

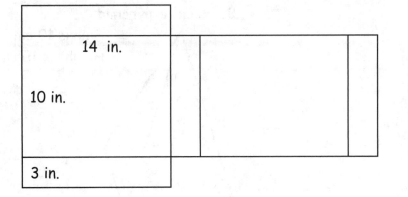

Surface Area = _____

11. Find the area of the given figure.

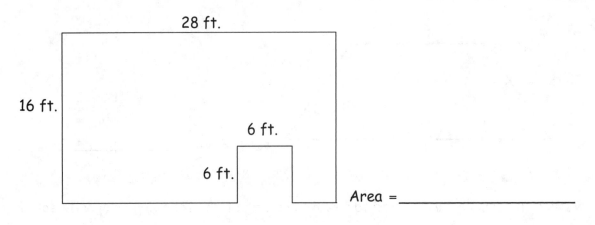

Area = _____

12. Find the missing measure. (Do not convert π to 3.14.)

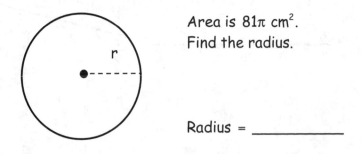

Area is 81π cm^2.
Find the radius.

Radius = _____

Measurement Review (cont.)

13. A rectangle with the dimensions of 6.3 cm and 5.8 cm is reduced by a scale factor of $\frac{1}{3}$. What are the dimensions of the new image? (Round to the nearest hundredth.)

14. A cylindrical can of punch has a volume of 120 fluid ounces. A second cylindrical can has dimensions that are $\frac{3}{5}$ the size of the larger can. Which is the closest volume of the smaller can?

   A. 26 fl. oz.   C. 72 fl. oz.

   B. 43 fl. oz.   D. 100 fl. oz.

15. Find the missing measure. (Do not convert π to 3.14.)

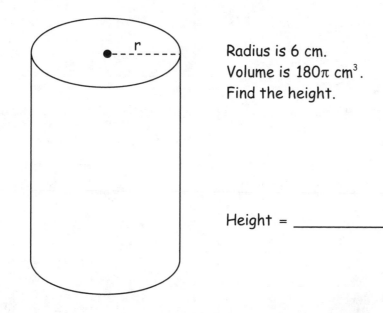

   Radius is 6 cm.
   Volume is 180π cm³.
   Find the height.

   Height = _____

Name _____

Proportions 2

Directions: Write proportions for the following and solve.

1. The freshman football team won 6 out of the 8 games they played last year. At this same rate, how many games will they win if they play 12 games this year?

   Record and bubble your answer below.

2. Mrs. Jamael ordered kitchen supplies from a mail order catalog. She received 9 out of 12 items ordered in one shipment. What percent of her order arrived?

   Record and bubble your answer below.

3. A box of cake mix that makes one cake calls for $\frac{3}{4}$ cup of water. How much water would be needed to make 54 cakes?

   Record and bubble your answer below.

Proportions 2 *(cont.)*

4. To paint the first wing at Edinburg High School, you would need 5 gallons of blue paint and 3 gallons of red paint. If it would take 120 gallons of paint to paint all the hallways in the school, how many gallons of blue paint would it take?

Record and bubble your answer below.

$\oplus$	⓪	⓪	⓪	⓪	⓪	•	⓪	⓪
$\ominus$	①	①	①	①	①		①	①
	②	②	②	②	②		②	②
	③	③	③	③	③		③	③
	④	④	④	④	④		④	④
	⑤	⑤	⑤	⑤	⑤		⑤	⑤
	⑥	⑥	⑥	⑥	⑥		⑥	⑥
	⑦	⑦	⑦	⑦	⑦		⑦	⑦
	⑧	⑧	⑧	⑧	⑧		⑧	⑧
	⑨	⑨	⑨	⑨	⑨		⑨	⑨

5. In a jewelry store, the ratio of rubies to opals is 3 to 2. If there are 150 rubies in the store, how many opals are there?

   A. 75 opals
   B. 100 opals
   C. 200 opals
   D. 225 opals

6. Tricia received an 8% commission on the sale of a digital phone package. The amount of the package was $50.00. How much commission did she earn?

   A. $1.00
   B. $2.00
   C. $3.00
   D. $4.00

7. On Wednesday, 9 out of 11 students attended tutorials. If 55 students were assigned tutorials, how many students did not attend tutorials?

   A. 10 students
   B. 12 students
   C. 30 students
   D. 40 students

Proportions 2 *(cont.)*

8. Cassandra bought a stereo with 80% of the money she received on her birthday. The stereo cost $219. How much money did Cassandra receive on her birthday?

   A. $36.53
   B. $250
   C. $273.75
   D. $17,520

9. In a zoo, the ratio of animals to caretakers is 6 to 1. If there is a total of 1,372 animals and caretakers in the zoo, how many are caretakers?

   A. 100 caretakers
   B. 196 caretakers
   C. 1,000 caretakers
   D. 1,176 caretakers

10. The average person has 32 teeth. If you have 32 teeth and 6 of them have fillings, what percent of your teeth do not have fillings?

    A. 18.75%
    B. 50.25%
    C. 75.50%
    D. 81.25%

11. Manny makes $405 every 9 days. At this rate, how much will he make in two weeks?

    A. $260.36
    B. $630
    C. $31
    D. $790

Name _____

Probability, Percent, and Proportion Review

1. Give the decimal value for each fraction.

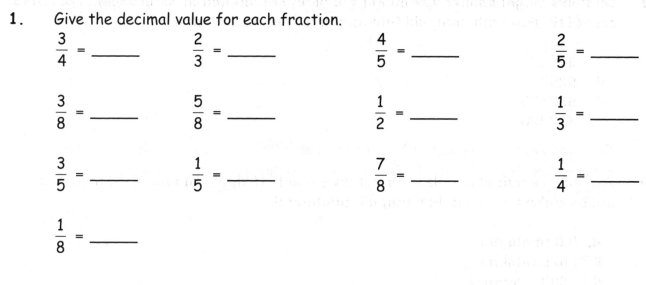

$\frac{3}{4}$ = _____ $\frac{2}{3}$ = _____ $\frac{4}{5}$ = _____ $\frac{2}{5}$ = _____

$\frac{3}{8}$ = _____ $\frac{5}{8}$ = _____ $\frac{1}{2}$ = _____ $\frac{1}{3}$ = _____

$\frac{3}{5}$ = _____ $\frac{1}{5}$ = _____ $\frac{7}{8}$ = _____ $\frac{1}{4}$ = _____

$\frac{1}{8}$ = _____

Directions: Calculate.

2. $3\frac{2}{5} \cdot 4$

3. $10 - 5\frac{1}{4}$

4. $3\frac{2}{3} + 4\frac{1}{4}$

5. The Rhodes insured their house for $78,400, which is 80% of the total value of the house. What is the value of their house?

    <u>Proportion</u>   <u>Solve</u>

6. A stereo was purchased at a discount of 25% for $187.50. What was the price of the stereo before the discount?

    <u>Proportion</u>   <u>Solve</u>

Probability, Percent, and Proportion Review (cont.)

7. Shameka scored 85% on a test, and 6 problems were wrong. How many problems were on the test?

   <u>Proportion</u>   <u>Solve</u>

8. Sean received a commission of 6% on the sale of a new house. If the amount of his commission was $6,300.00, what was the selling price of the house?

   <u>Proportion</u>   <u>Solve</u>

9. On Tuesday, Only Deals received a shipment of 240 Christmas trees. The manager had ordered 300 trees. What percent of her order arrived Tuesday?

   <u>Proportion</u>   <u>Solve</u>

10. Blake has 4 different baseball gloves, 3 different baseball bats, and 4 different baseballs. How many different combinations are there if he chooses 1 glove, 1 bat, and 1 ball?

    A. 11   C. 48
    B. 30   D. 36

11. If the digits can be repeated, how many 4-digit numbers can be formed using the digits 8, 3, 5, and 2?

    A. 64   C. 32
    B. 24   D. 256

Teacher Created Materials
PUBLISHING

#10623—Active Algebra—Algebra I, Guided Practice Book

Probability, Percent, and Proportion Review *(cont.)*

12. How many ways can four people be arranged in a row?

    A. 256   **C.** 64

    B. 32   **D.** 24

13. If the digits cannot be repeated, how many 3-digit numbers can be formed using only the digits 3, 8, 4, and 2?

    A. 64   **C.** 256

    B. 24   **D.** 32

14. A die and a coin are tossed. What is the probability of tossing a 5 and heads?

    A. $\dfrac{1}{4}$ **C.** $\dfrac{1}{12}$

    B. $\dfrac{1}{8}$ **D.** $\dfrac{1}{6}$

15. If 4 coins are tossed, what is the probability of tossing all heads?

    A. $\dfrac{1}{2}$ **C.** $\dfrac{1}{4}$

    B. $\dfrac{1}{16}$ **D.** $\dfrac{1}{8}$

16. Jamie can make 12 bows every hour. Which proportion will give the amount of bows Jamie can make in 20 hours?

    A. $\dfrac{12}{1}=\dfrac{x}{20}$ **C.** $\dfrac{12}{20}=\dfrac{1}{x}$

    B. $\dfrac{12}{1}=\dfrac{20}{x}$ **D.** $\dfrac{20}{12}=\dfrac{x}{1}$

Probability, Percent, and Proportion Review (cont.)

17. The Bruins scored 420 points after 5 games. If the team continues to score at this same rate, how many points will the team have scored after 30 games?

    <u>Proportion</u>   <u>Solve</u>

18. Tomicka can solve 18 out of every 20 equations correctly. At this rate, how many equations can she solve correctly if she solves 300 equations?

    <u>Proportion</u>   <u>Solve</u>

19. On the legend of a map, 3 inches represent 20 miles. How many inches are needed to represent 260 miles?

    <u>Proportion</u>   <u>Solve</u>

20. Kara's dog, Buddy, eats 4 cups of dog food every day. At this rate, how many cups of food will Buddy eat in 3 weeks?

    <u>Proportion</u>   <u>Solve</u>

Name _____

Solving for y Part 1

Directions: Solve for y.

1. $2x + 3y = 4$

2. $3x = 4y + 2$

3. $4y = 8x - 2$

4. $3y - 4x = 6$

5. $3x - 2y = 5$

6. $2x - 3 = 5y$

7. $6y = 2x - 3$

8. $4x - 3y = 10$

9. $3x - y = 4$

10. $6x - 3y = 8$

11. $4y = 8x + 3$

12. $7x = 5y + 2$

Name _____

Solving for *y* Part 2

Directions: Solve for *y*.

1. $3x + 12 = 6y$

2. $-6y + 4x = 8$

3. $8x + 10y = 11$

4. $2y - 3x = 4$

5. $5x + 12 = 8y$

6. $2y - x = 2$

7. $6x - y = -4$

8. $10x + 5y - 3 = 0$

9. $8x + 6y = -2$

10. $x + y = 2x + 3$

11. $4x - 9 = 3y$

12. $2y - x = -9$

Teacher Created Materials
PUBLISHING

Name _____

Functions, Domains, and Ranges

Directions: State the relation as a set of ordered pairs. Determine the domain and range of the relation.

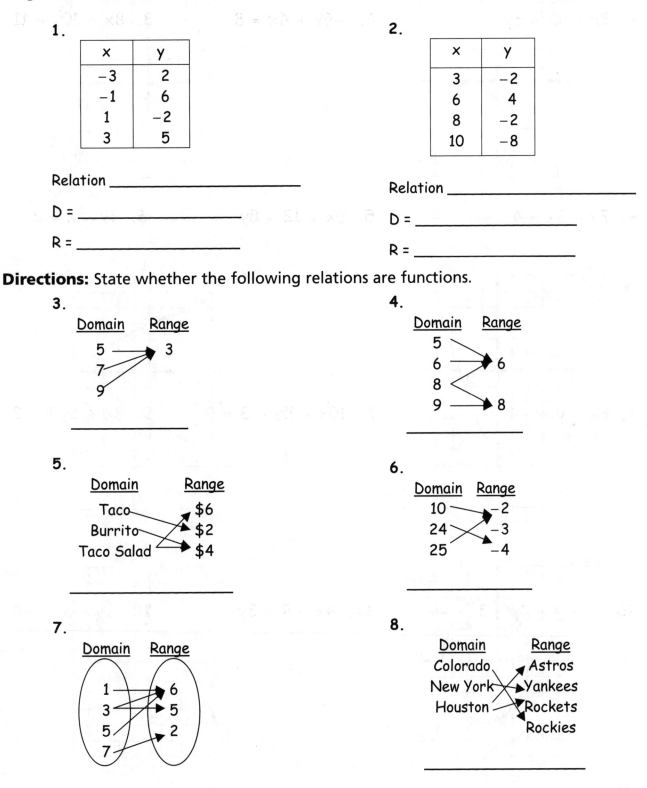

1.

x	y
−3	2
−1	6
1	−2
3	5

Relation _____

D = _____

R = _____

2.

x	y
3	−2
6	4
8	−2
10	−8

Relation _____

D = _____

R = _____

Directions: State whether the following relations are functions.

3.

Domain   Range

5 → 3
7
9

_____

4.

Domain   Range

5
6 → 6
8
9 → 8

_____

5.

Domain   Range

Taco $6
Burrito $2
Taco Salad $4

_____

6.

Domain   Range

10 → −2
24 → −3
25 → −4

_____

7.

Domain   Range

1   6
3   5
5   2
7

_____

8.

Domain   Range

Colorado   Astros
New York   Yankees
Houston   Rockets
   Rockies

_____

Functions, Domains, and Ranges *(cont.)*

Directions: Use the vertical line test to determine which of the following graphs are functions. Write "yes" if the graph is a function and "no" if the graph is not a function.

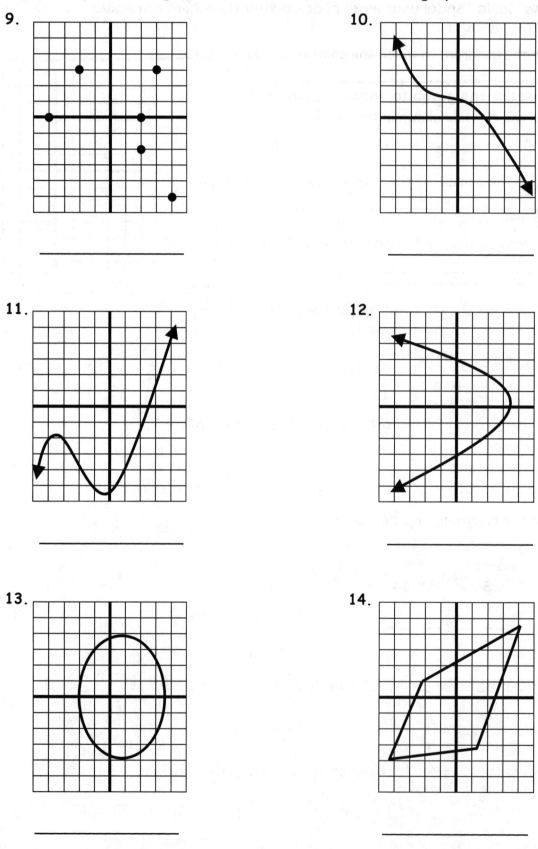

9.

10.

_____

_____

11.

12.

_____

_____

13.

14.

_____

_____

Teacher Created Materials
PUBLISHING

Name _____

Graphing Mid-Unit Review

Directions: Solve. Show your work neatly on another sheet of paper.

1. Name the quadrant in which the point $(-1, -3)$ is located.

   _____

Directions: Use the graph to answer questions 2–4.

2. State the relation shown in the graph.

   _____

3. What is the domain of the relation shown in the graph?

   _____

4. What is the range of the relation shown in the graph?

   _____

5. What are the domain and range of the relation shown in the table on the right?

x	y
2	3
4	5

   A. D = {2, 3}   R = {4, 5}   **C.** D = {2, 5}   R = {3, 4}   5._____

   B. D = {2, 4}   R = {3, 5}   **D.** D = {3, 2}   R = {5, 4}

6. What is the graph of the set of ordered pairs (c, 0), where "c" is any number?

   A. the y-axis   **C.** the origin   6._____

   B. the x-axis   **D.** cannot be determined

7. Solve the equation $4x - 2y = 6$ for "y."

   A. $y = -2x - 3$ **B.** $y = 5x$ **C.** $y = -2x$ **D.** $y = 2x - 3$ 7._____

8. Solve the equation $3a + 4m = 6$ for "m."

   A. $m = \frac{3}{4}a + \frac{3}{2}$ **C.** $m = -\frac{3}{4}a + \frac{3}{2}$ 8._____

   B. $m = -\frac{3}{4}a - \frac{3}{2}$ **D.** $m = \frac{9a}{4}$

9. What is the domain of the relation shown in the mapping?

   A. {3, 4, 5, 6}   **C.** {-2, 3, -1, 5}   9._____

   B. {-2, -1, 0, 1}   **D.** {0, 4, 1, 6}

10. What is the range of the solution set of the equation $2c + 4d = 8$ if the domain is {-2, 0, 2}?

    A. {4, 6, 8}   **B.** {1, 2, 3}   **C.** {-1, -2, -3}   **D.** {0, 4, 8}   10._____

 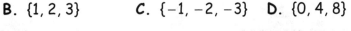

Graphing Mid-Unit Review (cont.)

11. What is the domain of the solution set of the equation $3r - 6s = 6$ when the range is { $-3, 0, 3$ }?

    A. {$-8, -2, 4$}   B. {$-\dfrac{5}{2}, -1, \dfrac{1}{2}$}   C. {$-4, 2, 8$}   D. {$-3, 0, 3$}   11._____

12. Which equation is a linear equation?

    A. $y = x^3$ B. $y = \dfrac{1}{x}$ C. $y = 2x + 3$ D. $x^2 + y^2 = 9$ 12._____

13. Determine which relation is a function.   13._____

    A.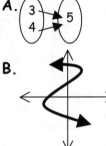

    C.

x	y
6	5
7	5
7	6

    B.

    D. {($2, 3$) ($2, 6$)}

14. Determine which relation is a function.

    A. {($2, 5$) ($3, 5$) ($6, 5$)}   C. {($1, 7$) ($2, 8$) ($1, 9$)}   14._____
    B. {($2, 3$) ($2, 6$) ($2, 8$)}   D.

15. If $f(x) = 3x - 2$, what is the value of $f(-2)$?

    A. 0   B. 4   C. -8 D. 8   15._____

16. If $g(x) = 2x^2 - 3x$, what is the value of $g(-1)$?

    A. 1   B. 5   C. -7 D. 7   16._____

17. Which equation represents the function?

    A. $y = x + 6$ C. $y = 2x - 4$
    B. $y = 2x + 4$ D. $y = 3x + 4$

x	1	3	5	7	9
y	6	10	14	18	22

    17._____

18. Which equation represents the function?

    A. $y = -5x + 2$ C. $y = 4x - 1$
    B. $y = 3x - 2$ D. $y = -3x + 2$

x	-4	-1	0	2	3
y	14	5	2	-4	-7

    18._____

19. Which equation represents the function?

    A. $y = \dfrac{1}{3}x - 2$ C. $y = 3x + 2$

    B. $y = 3x - 2$ D. $y = -\dfrac{1}{3}x - 2$

x	0	3	6	9	12
y	-2	-3	-4	-5	-6

    19._____

Name _____

Measurement Review (Mid-Unit Graphing)

Directions: Solve the following problems.

1. Find the volume of the following shape.

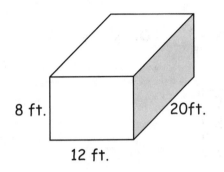

Volume = _____

2. Find the volume of the following shape.

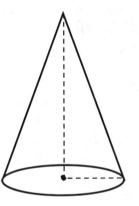

Height is 12 in.
Diameter is 18 in.

Volume = _____

3. Find the area of the following shape.

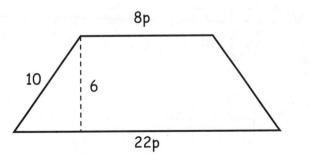

Area = _____

Measurement Review (Mid-Unit Graphing) *(cont.)*

4. Which formula can be used to find the volume of the following composite solid?

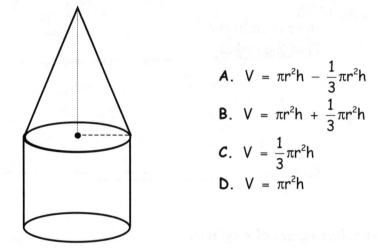

 A. $V = \pi r^2 h - \dfrac{1}{3}\pi r^2 h$

 B. $V = \pi r^2 h + \dfrac{1}{3}\pi r^2 h$

 C. $V = \dfrac{1}{3}\pi r^2 h$

 D. $V = \pi r^2 h$

5. Reginald made a stand out of cinder block for his science project, like the one shown below. Find the volume, in cubic inches, of the cinder block. Exclude the volume of the holes.

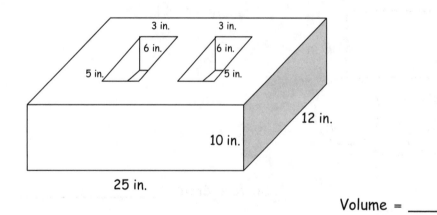

 Volume = _____

6. Find the surface area of the following net of a rectangular prism.

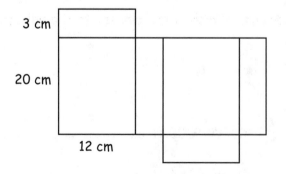

 Surface Area = _____

Teacher Created Materials
PUBLISHING

#10623—Active Algebra—Algebra I, Guided Practice Book

Measurement Review (Mid-Unit Graphing) *(cont.)*

7. Find the missing measure. (Do not use 3.14 for π.)

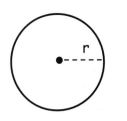

Area is 169π cm^2.
Find the radius.

Radius = _____

8. Find the surface area of the following net of a cylinder.

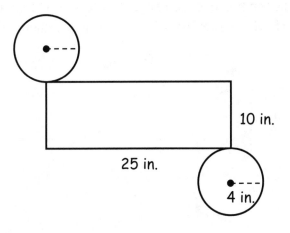

10 in.

25 in.

4 in.

Surface Area = _____

9. A cylindrical can of cleaner has a volume of 620 fluid ounces. A second cylindrical can has dimensions that are $\frac{2}{3}$ the size of the larger can. Which is the closest to the volume of the smaller can?

A. V = 425 fl. oz.

C. V = 300 fl. oz.

B. V = 275 fl. oz.

D. V = 184 fl. oz.

Measurement Review (Mid-Unit Graphing) *(cont.)*

10. A manufacturing company sells two products that are shipped in cartons shaped like rectangular prisms.

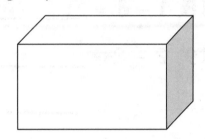 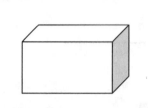

The larger carton has a volume of 1,200 cubic inches. The smaller carton has dimensions that are one-third the size of the large carton. What is the volume, in cubic inches, of the smaller carton? (Round to the nearest cubic inch.)

Volume = _____

Name _____

Adding Integers (for Slope)

Directions: Solve.

1. $-1 + -6 =$ _____

2. $-4 - 1 =$ _____

3. $4 - (-2) =$ _____

4. $4 - 6 =$ _____

5. $2 - (-1) =$ _____

6. $3 + 2 =$ _____

7. $4 - (-1) =$ _____

8. $-3 + -2 =$ _____

9. $-4 - 1 =$ _____

10. $-1 - 1 =$ _____

11. $-2 + 3 =$ _____

12. $-4 - (-2) =$ _____

13. $-2 - 3 =$ _____

14. $6 - 5 =$ _____

15. $3 - 4 =$ _____

16. $-2 - 2 =$ _____

17. $-5 - 1 =$ _____

18. $1 - 3 =$ _____

19. $2 - 2 =$ _____

20. $3 - 1 =$ _____

21. $1 - (-3) =$ _____

22. $-2 - (-4) =$ _____

23. $-3 + 5 =$ _____

24. $6 - (-2) =$ _____

25. $5 - 6 =$ _____

26. $3 - 4 =$ _____

27. $-3 - 4 =$ _____

28. $-1 + -4 =$ _____

29. $-3 - (-5) =$ _____

30. $-3 + 6 =$ _____

31. $-6 - (-9) =$ _____

32. $0 - (-8) =$ _____

33. $3 - (-2) =$ _____

34. $-7 - (-8) =$ _____

Name _____

Slope 1

Directions: Write each ordered pair, and count the slope.

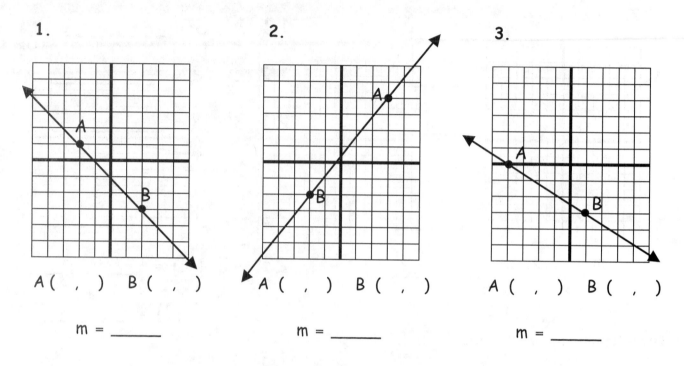

1.

A (,) B (,)

m = _____

2.

A (,) B (,)

m = _____

3.

A (,) B (,)

m = _____

Directions: Choose two points, and count each slope.

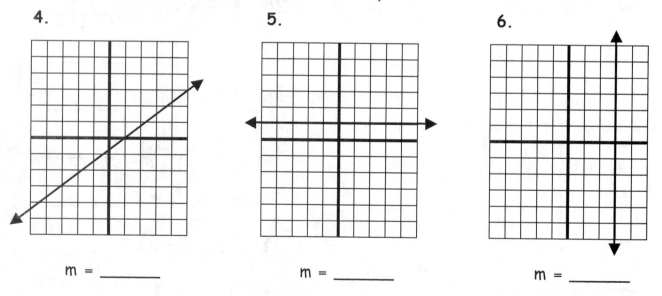

4.

m = _____

5.

m = _____

6.

m = _____

Slope 1 (cont.)

Directions: Choose two points, and count each slope.

7.

8.

9.

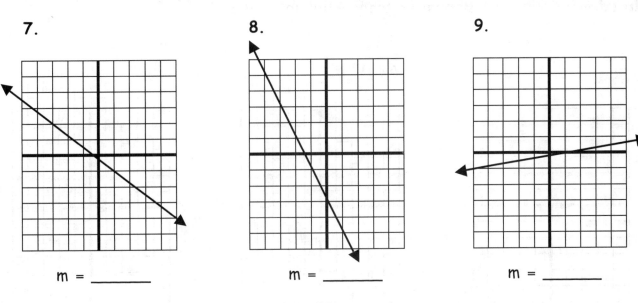

m = _____   m = _____   m = _____

Directions: Find each slope using the slope formula. $\left(m = \dfrac{y_2 - y_1}{x_2 - x_1} \right)$

$(x_1, y_1) \quad (x_2, y_2)$

10. $(3, 5) \quad (0, 1)$ **11.** $(4, 5) \; (1, 3)$ **12.** $(4, 2) \; (0, 3)$

Directions: Plot the points, draw each line, and find the slope. $\left(\dfrac{rise}{run} \right)$

13. $A(3, 5) \quad B(0, 1)$ **14.** $A(4, 5) \quad B(1, 3)$ **15.** $A(4, 2) \quad B(0, 3)$

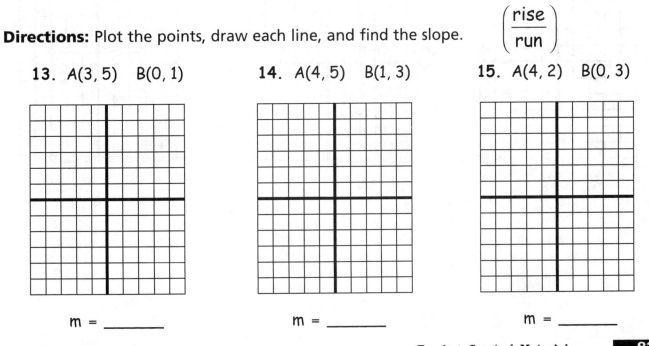

m = _____   m = _____   m = _____

Name _____

Slope 2

Directions: Count each slope from the given point.

1. $m = -\dfrac{2}{3}$

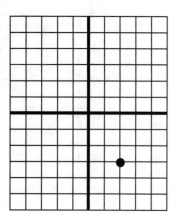

2. $m = -\dfrac{1}{2}$

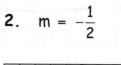

3. $m = 5$

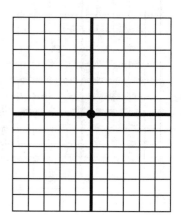

4. $m = -3$

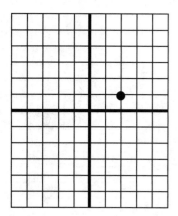

5. $m = \dfrac{1}{4}$

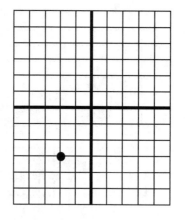

6. $m = -\dfrac{1}{3}$

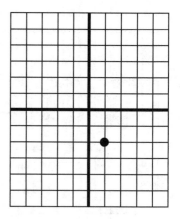

Slope 2 (cont.)

Directions: Plot the points, count the slope, and draw each line.

7. $(0, 2)$ $m = 3$ **8.** $(-1, 3)$ $m = \dfrac{2}{3}$ **9.** $(2, 3)$ $m = -2$

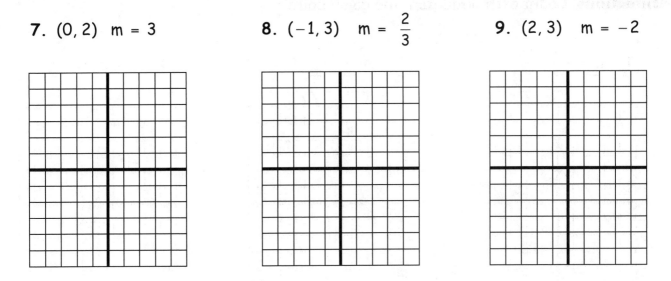

Directions: Plot the points, draw each line, and then count each slope.

10. $(3, 5)$ $(4, 5)$ **11.** $(3, 1)$ $(3, 2)$ **12.** $(2, -1)$ $(-1, -1)$

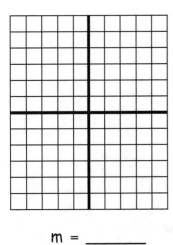 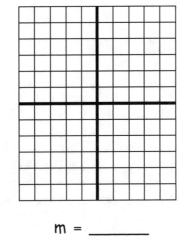 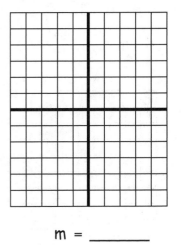

  m = _____   m = _____   m = _____

Directions: Find each slope using the slope formula. $\left(m = \dfrac{y_2 - y_1}{x_2 - x_1} \right)$

  (x_1, y_1) (x_2, y_2)

13. $(-6, 4)$ $(3, -1)$ **14.** $(2, 3)$ $(2, 6)$ **15.** $(2, 3)$ $(4, -6)$

Name _____

Slope 3

Directions: Find each ordered pair, and count the slope.

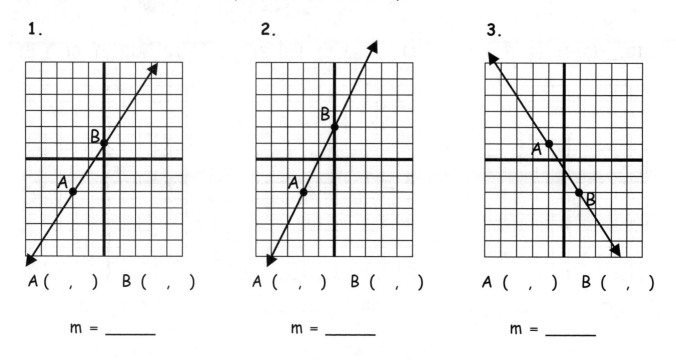

1.

A (,) B (,)

m = _____

2.

A (,) B (,)

m = _____

3.

A (,) B (,)

m = _____

Directions: Choose two points, and count each slope.

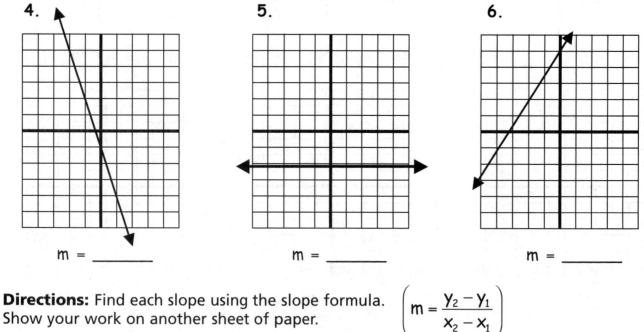

4.

m = _____

5.

m = _____

6.

m = _____

Directions: Find each slope using the slope formula. $\left(m = \dfrac{y_2 - y_1}{x_2 - x_1} \right)$
Show your work on another sheet of paper.

(x_1, y_1) (x_2, y_2)

7. (3, 5) (2, 5)

8. (−4, 5) (−3, 2)

9. (4, 2) (4, 6)

Slope 3 (cont.)

Directions: Plot the points, draw each line, and find each slope. $\left(\dfrac{\text{rise}}{\text{run}}\right)$

10. $A(3, 4)$ $B(-2, 3)$

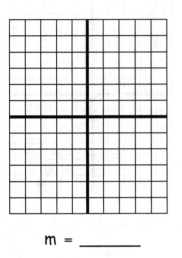

m = _____

11. $A(-3, 5)$ $B(0, 2)$

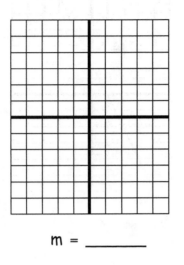

m = _____

12. $A(3, 2)$ $B(-1, 5)$

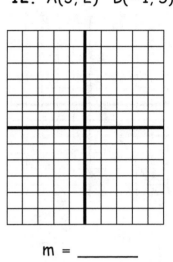

m = _____

13. $A(5, 0)$ $B(5, -3)$

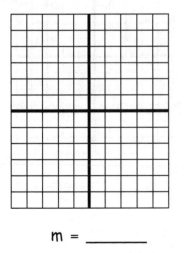

m = _____

14. $A(-3, 2)$ $B(-2, 3)$

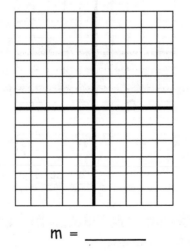

m = _____

15. $A(4, 4)$ $B(-2, 4)$

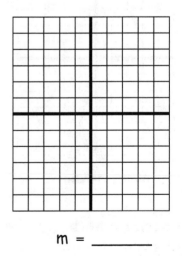

m = _____

Name _____

Slope 4

Directions: Count each slope.

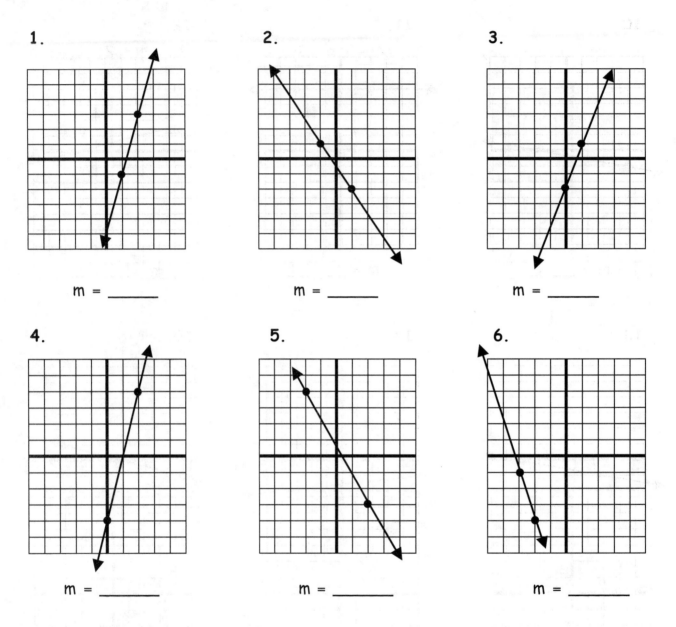

1.

m = _____

2.

m = _____

3.

m = _____

4.

m = _____

5.

m = _____

6.

m = _____

7. Are the slopes of the above lines considered steep or flat?_____

8. Why do the lines in #2, #5, and #6 slant to the left?_____

9. Why do the lines in #1, #3, and #4 slant to the right?_____

Slope 4 (cont.)

Directions: Count each slope.

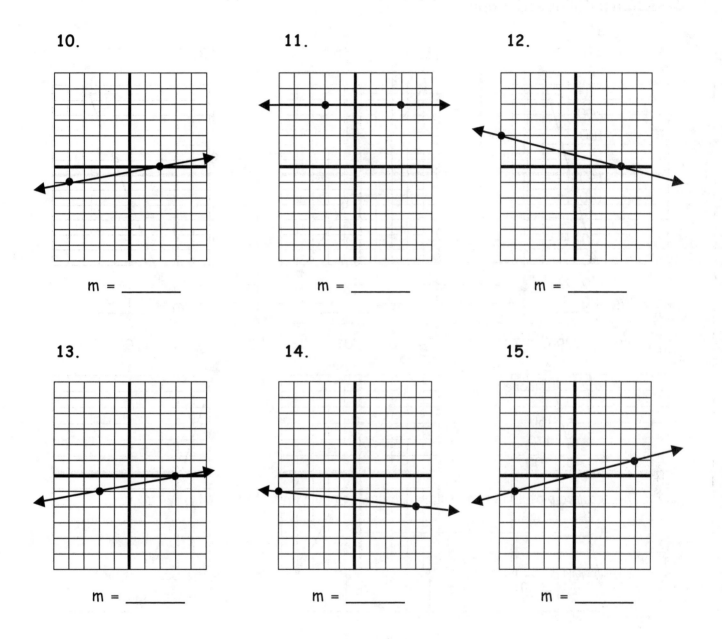

10.

m = _____

11.

m = _____

12.

m = _____

13.

m = _____

14.

m = _____

15.

m = _____

16. Are the slopes of the above lines considered steep or flat? _____

17. What characteristic of the slope makes a line steep or flat?

_____

Name _____

Scatter Plots Packet

1. The graph below shows the sale of CDs in millions 1996–2005.

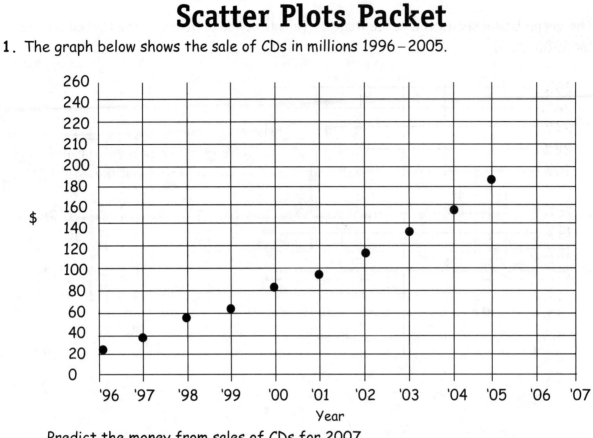

Predict the money from sales of CDs for 2007.

A. 160   D. 240
B. 170   E. 260
C. 200

2. The scatter plot shows the sales at a new company over the last few years.

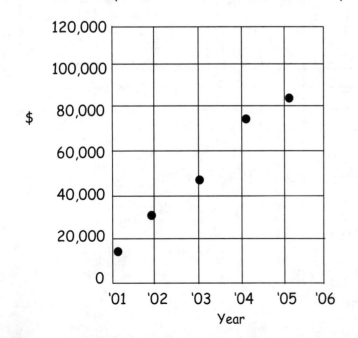

Which is the best estimate for the expected sales for 2006?

A. 120,000   D. 125,000
B. 90,000   E. 100,000
C. 80,000

Scatter Plots Packet (cont.)

3. The graph below shows the percentage of female police officers in the United States for 1980–2000.

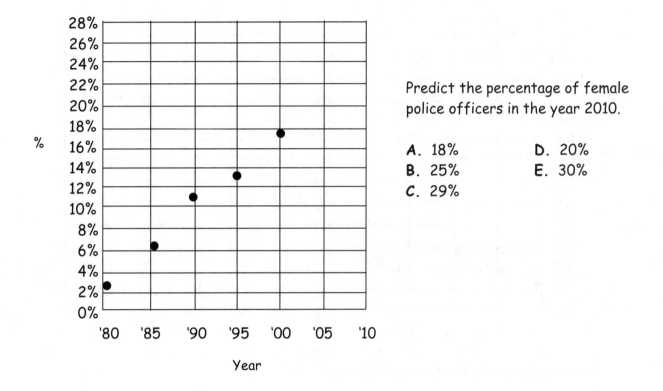

Predict the percentage of female police officers in the year 2010.

A. 18%   D. 20%
B. 25%   E. 30%
C. 29%

4. The scatter plot shows the year-to-date expenditures for teacher supplies at Warren High School.

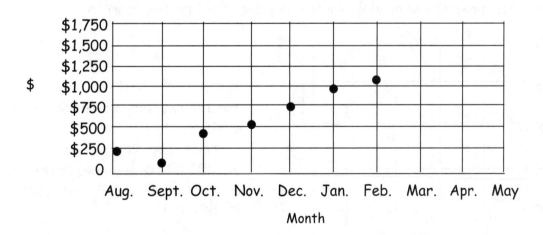

Predict the high school's end-of-year (May) total expenditures.

A. $1,850   D. $1,600
B. $1,175   E. $1,000
C. $2,000

Scatter Plots Packet *(cont.)*

5. LeBron is shooting free throws after school. The graph shows the total number of free throws he has made so far.

Number of Free Throws Made

Number of Minutes

Predict the total number of free throws LeBron will make in 45 minutes.
- **A.** 80
- **B.** 90
- **C.** 100
- **D.** 110
- **E.** 120

6. Carlos started an exercise program in January. He kept a record of how many sit-ups he did each day.

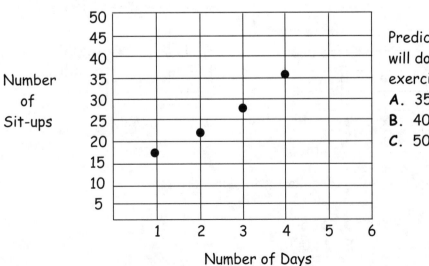

Number of Sit-ups

Number of Days

Predict how many sit-ups Carlos will do on the 6th day of his exercise program.
- **A.** 35
- **B.** 40
- **C.** 50
- **D.** 60
- **E.** 70

Scatter Plots Packet *(cont.)*

7. The graph below shows the average selling price of vehicles from 2000 to 2007.

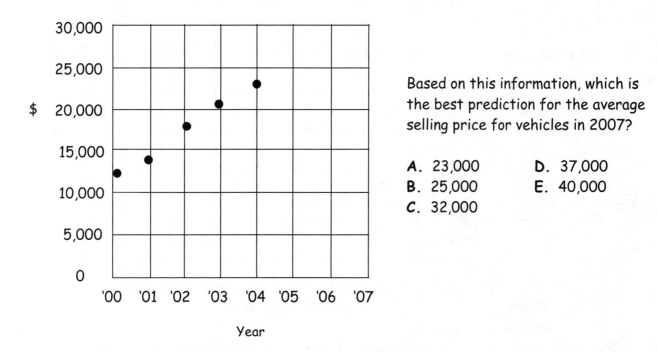

Based on this information, which is the best prediction for the average selling price for vehicles in 2007?

A. 23,000   **D.** 37,000
B. 25,000   **E.** 40,000
C. 32,000

8. Daniel mows grass during the summer to earn money. The graph below shows the total number of lawns mowed so far.

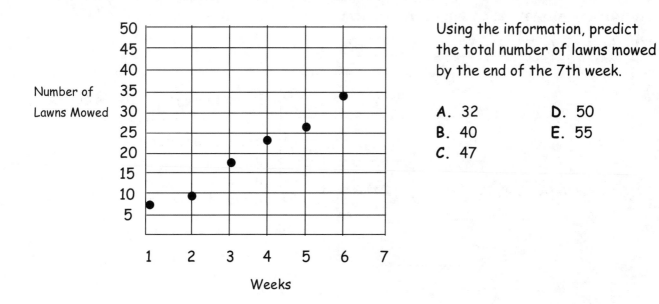

Using the information, predict the total number of lawns mowed by the end of the 7th week.

A. 32   **D.** 50
B. 40   **E.** 55
C. 47

    Teacher Created Materials PUBLISHING   **93**

Name _____

Solving for *y* and Slope Review

Directions: Solve for *y*.

1. $2x + 3y = 6$

2. $3x = 4y - 10$

3. $-6y = 2x + 1$

4. $3y + 6x = -8$

5. $-4x - 5 = 6y$

6. $-3x = 7y + 7$

7. $-2x = 3y - 15$

8. $2y = -6x - 4$

9. $-3x - 5y = 10$

Directions: Calculate each slope. When applicable, state if the slopes are undefined.

10. $(-3, 5)\,(-2, 6)$

11. $(3, -2)\,(3, 0)$

12. $(-6, 4)\,(-8, -2)$

13. $(4, -3)\,(6, -3)$

14. $(-5, 1)\,(0, -2)$

15. $(-3, 2)\,(-6, -1)$

Solving for *y* and Slope Review (cont.)

Directions: Write each ordered pair, and then count each slope.

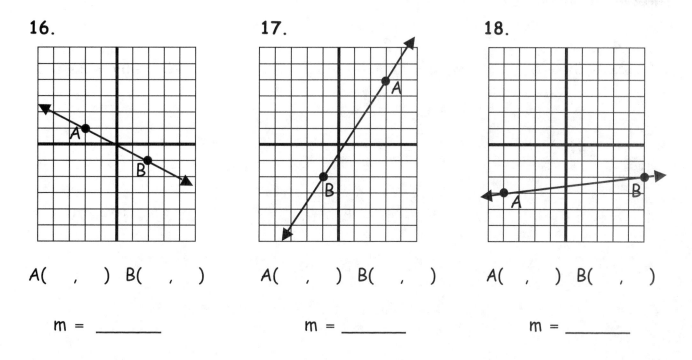

16.

A(,   ) B(,   )

m = _____

17.

A(,   ) B(,   )

m = _____

18.

A(,   ) B(,   )

m = _____

Directions: Choose two points and count each slope.

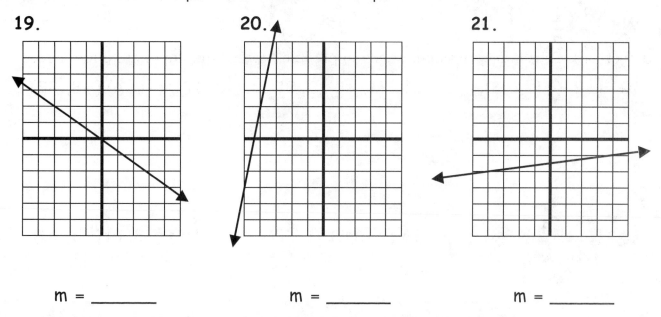

19.

m = _____

20.

m = _____

21.

m = _____

Name _____

Fractions Review

Directions: Solve.

1. $\dfrac{4}{3}(5) - 8$

2. $\dfrac{2}{5} \div 3 - 6$

3. $-\dfrac{2}{3}(4) + 6$

4. $5 \div \left(-\dfrac{1}{2}\right) + 3$

5. $-\dfrac{3}{2}(6) - 4$

6. $7 \div \left(-\dfrac{3}{2}\right) + 2$

7. $-\dfrac{3}{4}\left(\dfrac{1}{2}\right) - \dfrac{1}{3}$

8. $-\dfrac{3}{7}(2) + \dfrac{2}{7}$

9. $-\dfrac{1}{6}\left(\dfrac{4}{5}\right) + 3$

10. $-\dfrac{1}{5}\left(\dfrac{4}{3}\right) - 6$

11. $-3 \div \left(-\dfrac{4}{7}\right) + 2$

12. $\dfrac{1}{8}\left(-\dfrac{3}{2}\right) - 3$

Teacher Created Materials
PUBLISHING

Fractions Review *(cont.)*

13. $-6 \div \dfrac{1}{2} - 3$

14. $2\left(\dfrac{3}{2}\right) - 5$

15. $\dfrac{4}{5}\left(\dfrac{3}{8}\right) - \dfrac{5}{3}$

16. $-10 \div \dfrac{2}{3} - 7$

17. $-\dfrac{8}{9}\left(\dfrac{3}{4}\right) - 7$

18. $8 - \dfrac{1}{4}\left(\dfrac{2}{3}\right)$

19. $-6 - 3 \div \dfrac{1}{3}$

20. $-4\left(-\dfrac{1}{2}\right) + \dfrac{3}{4}$

Bonus: Solve.

$$\dfrac{\dfrac{3}{8}\left(\dfrac{2}{5}\right) - 3}{-\dfrac{1}{4}\left(\dfrac{7}{5}\right) - \dfrac{5}{2}}$$

Name _____

Writing Equations of Lines

Directions: Write the equation of each line using point-slope form, then solve for *y*.

$$y - y_1 = m(x - x_1)$$

1. $(1, -3)$ $m = -2$

2. $(-2, 4) (-3, 6)$

Directions: Write the equation of each line using slope-intercept form.

$$y = mx + b$$

3. $(1, -3)$ $m = -2$

4. $(-2, 4) (-3, 6)$

Directions: Use either form to write an equation of each line.

5. $(-4, 8)$ $m = -\dfrac{1}{3}$

6. $(-3, 6) (4, -2)$

Writing Equations of Lines (cont.)

Directions: Write an equation of each line with the given information.

7. $(3, -2)$ m = undefined

8. $(-2, 3) (6, 3)$

9. m = 3, b = -6

10. m = $\frac{2}{3}$, x-intercept of 4

11. m = $\frac{3}{4}$, y-intercept of 2

12. $(4, -2) (6, -2)$

13. m = $-\frac{1}{3}$, b = 5

14. $(5, -3)$ m = undefined

Teacher Created Materials
PUBLISHING

Name _____

Graphing 1

Directions: Find the *y*-intercept, slope, and equation of each line.

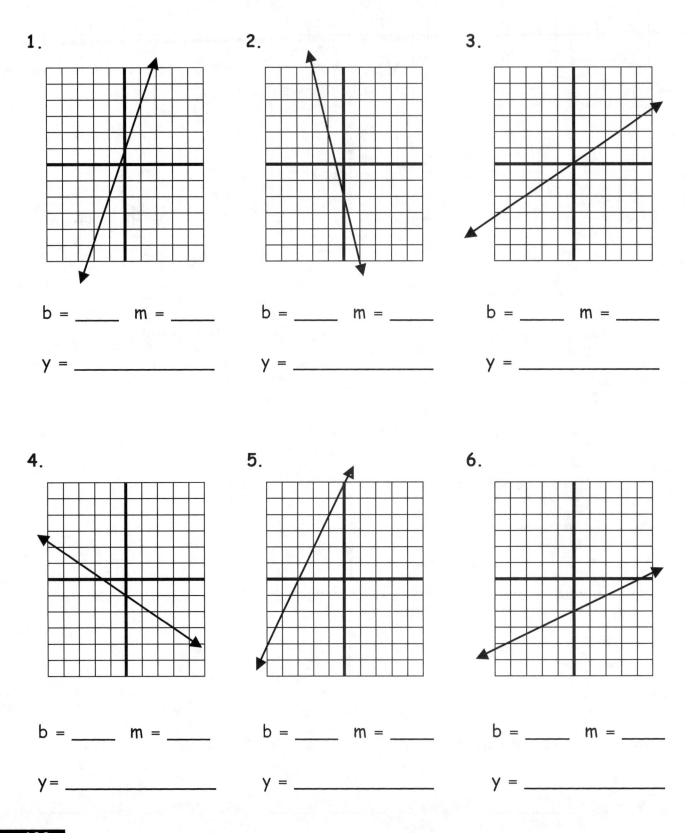

1.

b = _____   m = _____

y = _____

2.

b = _____   m = _____

y = _____

3.

b = _____   m = _____

y = _____

4.

b = _____   m = _____

y = _____

5.

b = _____   m = _____

y = _____

6.

b = _____   m = _____

y = _____

   #10623—Active Algebra—Algebra I, Guided Practice Book

Graphing 1 *(cont.)*

Directions: Graph each line using the given information, and write an equation.

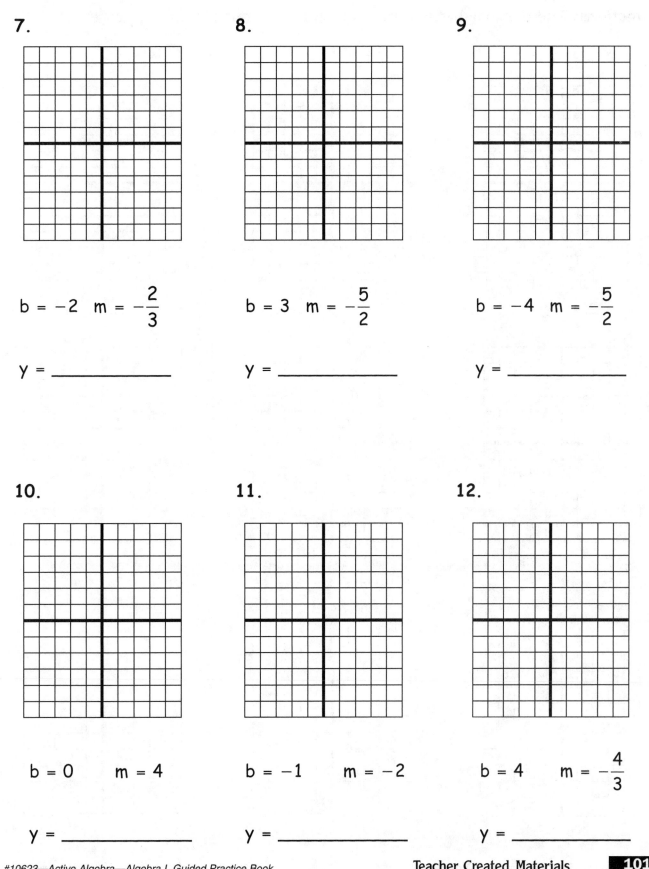

7.

$b = -2 \quad m = -\dfrac{2}{3}$

y = _____

8.

$b = 3 \quad m = -\dfrac{5}{2}$

y = _____

9.

$b = -4 \quad m = -\dfrac{5}{2}$

y = _____

10.

$b = 0 \qquad m = 4$

y = _____

11.

$b = -1 \qquad m = -2$

y = _____

12.

$b = 4 \qquad m = -\dfrac{4}{3}$

y = _____

Teacher Created Materials
PUBLISHING

Name _____

Graphing 2

Directions: Graph each linear equation, and label the slope and the *y*-intercept.

1. x + 3 = 0

2. y = −2

3. x = 4

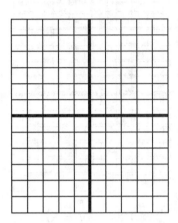
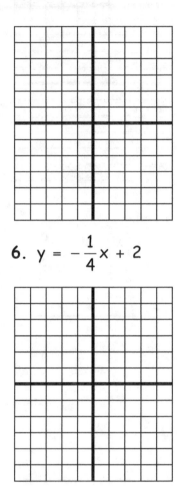

4. y − 3 = 0

5. y = $\frac{1}{2}$x − 3

6. y = −$\frac{1}{4}$x + 2

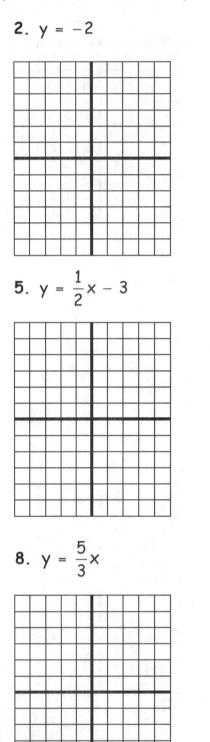

7. y = 4x − 2

8. y = $\frac{5}{3}$x

9. y = 2x − 4

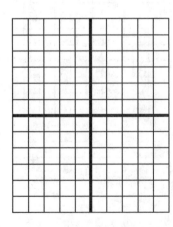
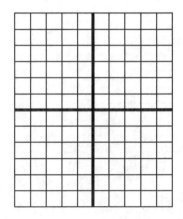

Graphing 2 *(cont.)*

10. $2x + y = -3$

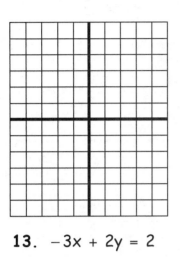

11. $2x + 3y = 6$

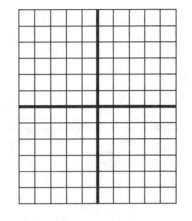

12. $3x + 4y = 12$

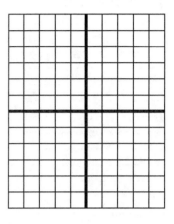

13. $-3x + 2y = 2$

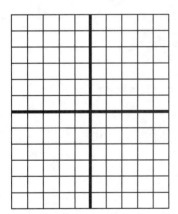

14. $3x - y = 1$

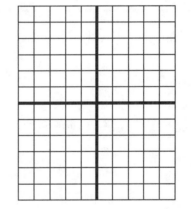

15. $4x + 3y = 0$

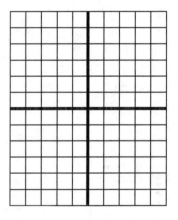

16. $6x - 5y + 20 = 0$

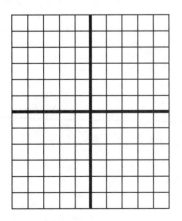

17. $x - 4y = 8$

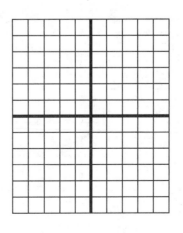

18. $2x - 2y + 6 = 0$

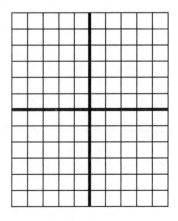

Name _____

Parameter Changes Packet

Directions: Complete the following exercises using your graphing calculator.

1. Enter $y = x$ as y_1 in your graphing calculator and leave it until further notice.
   Sketch and label what you see on the graph below.

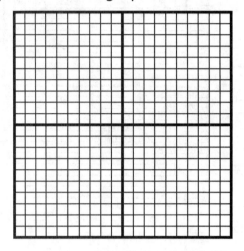

This graph is called the "PARENT FORM" of an equation.

2. What is the coefficient of x in $y = x$? _____ What is the constant? _____

3. Does this coefficient represent the slope or the y-intercept of the line? _____

4. Enter $y = -x$ as y_2 in your graphing calculator.
   Sketch and label what you see on the graph below.

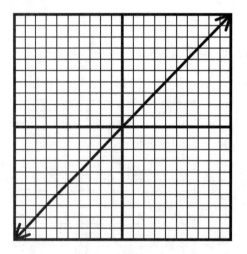

5. How did $y = -x$ change in relation to $y = x$? (Hint: How did the slope change?)

_____

Parameter Changes Packet *(cont.)*

CLEAR y_2 AT THIS TIME

6. Enter y = 3x as y_2 in your graphing calculator.
   Sketch and label what you see on the graph below.

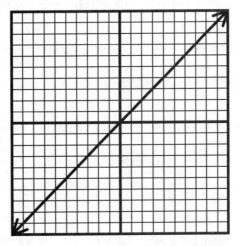

7. How did y = 3x change in relation to y = x? (Hint: What happened to the slope?)

   _____

8. Enter y = 7x as y_3 in your graphing calculator.
   Sketch and label this new line on the same graph you used for question #6.

9. How did the slope of this line change in relation to the other two lines?

   _____

10. To graph a line flatter than y = x, what type of number must the coefficient
    of x be? (Hint: You must have more "run" than "rise.") _____

CLEAR y_2 AND y_3 AT THIS TIME

11. Enter y = $\frac{1}{2}$x as y_2 in your graphing calculator.

    Sketch and label what you see on the graph below.

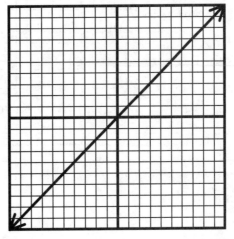

Parameter Changes Packet *(cont.)*

12. How did the slope of this line change in relation to the "parent form?"

_____

13. Enter y = $\frac{1}{5}$ x as y_3 in your graphing calculator.

Sketch and label what you see on the same graph you used for question #11.

14. How did the slope of this line change in relation to the other two lines?

_____

15. What is the y-intercept of the "parent form," y = x? _____

CLEAR y_2 AND y_3 AT THIS TIME

16. Enter y = x + 3 as y_2 in your graphing calculator.
Sketch and label what you see on the graph below.

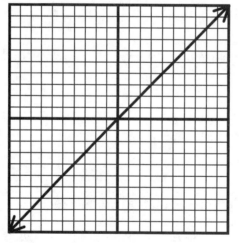

17. What is the coefficient of x in y = x + 3?_____ What is the constant?_____

18. What does the constant represent? _____

19. How did the graph of this line change in relation to the "parent form"? (Hint: Did the line shift up or down?)

_____

20. What caused this line to shift? _____

#10623—Active Algebra—Algebra I, Guided Practice Book

Parameter Changes Packet *(cont.)*

21. Enter $y = x + 7$ as y_3 in your graphing calculator.
Sketch and label what you see on the same graph you used for #16.

_____

22. How did the graph of this line change in relation to the other two lines?

_____

23. What can we say happens to a line when the constant is positive?

_____

24. What will happen to the line when the equation has a negative constant?

_____

CLEAR y_2 AND y_3 AT THIS TIME

25. Enter $y = x - 2$ as y_2 in your graphing calculator.
Sketch and label what you see on the graph below.

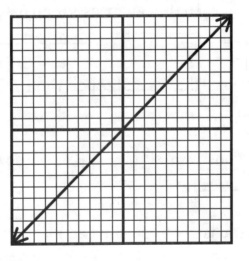

26. What happened to the "parent form" when a negative constant was added?

_____

27. Based on the activity you have just done, what determines the slant (or steepness) of a line? _____
What determines the shift? _____

Teacher Created Materials
PUBLISHING

Parameter Changes Packet *(cont.)*

Directions: Write equations to match the following parameter changes. Then, use your graphing calculator to check the equations.

28. Write two equations that shift $y = x$ up the y-axis.

   _____   _____

29. Write two equations that shift $y = x$ down the y-axis.

   _____   _____

30. Write two equations that slant to the right.

   _____   _____

31. Write two equations that slant to the left.

   _____   _____

32. Write two equations that are steeper than $y = x$.

   _____   _____

33. Write two equations that are not as steep as $y = x$.

   _____   _____

34. Write two equations that are steeper than $y = x$ and slant to the left.

   _____   _____

35. Write two equations that shift $y = 2x - 3$ down the y-axis.

   _____   _____

36. Write two equations that are shifted up the y-axis and are flatter than $y = 4x + 1$.

   _____   _____

37. Write two equations that are parallel to each other.

   _____   _____

Name _____

Parameter Changes Review

Directions: Write equations to match the following parameter changes. All of your answers must be different than what you did on the last page of the *Parameter Changes Packet* (page 108). Then, use your graphing calculator to check the equations.

1. Write two equations that shift $y = x$ up the y-axis.

    _____   _____

2. Write two equations that shift $y = x$ down the y-axis.

    _____   _____

3. Write two equations that slant to the right.

    _____   _____

4. Write two equations that slant to the left.

    _____   _____

5. Write two equations that are steeper than $y = x$.

    _____   _____

6. Write two equations that are not as steep as $y = x$.

    _____   _____

7. Write two equations that are steeper than $y = x$ and slant to the left.

    _____   _____

8. Write two equations that shift $y = 3x + 2$ down the y-axis.

    _____   _____

9. Write two equations that are shifted up the y–axis and are not as steep as $y = 5x - 4$.

    _____   _____

10. Write two equations that are parallel to each other.

    _____   _____

Name _____

Graphing Unit Review 1

Directions: Show your work neatly on another piece of paper.

1. Write the equation of the line passing through the points (2, 2) and (2, 5).   1. _____
   A. y = 2   B. y = 3   C. x = 2   D. y = 5

2. Write the equation of the line passing through the points (−1, 4) and (2, 4).   2. _____
   A. y = 4   B. y = −1   C. x = 2   D. x = 4

3. Draw and label the line x = 3.   4. Draw and label the line y = −2.

5. What is the slope of the line passing through (−2, 3) and (−3, 1)?   5. _____
   A. $-\dfrac{2}{5}$ B. −2   C. $\dfrac{2}{5}$ D. 2

6. Find the slope and the y−intercept of the line below.   6. _____

   A. m = 1   B. m = $\dfrac{1}{3}$

      b = $\dfrac{1}{3}$ b = 1

   C. m = 3   D. m = 1
      b = 1   b = 3

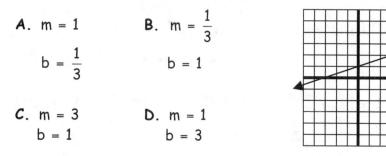

7. Find the equation of the line that passes through (−2, 1) with the slope of 0.   7. _____
   A. y = 1   B. y = −2   C. x = −2   D. x = 1

8. What is the equation of the line whose graph has a slope of −3 and   8. _____
   a y-intercept of 2?
   A. y = −3x + 2   C. y = −2x + 1
   B. y = 2x − 3   D. y = 3x − 2

9. Find the equation of the line passing through (−2, 4) with an undefined slope.   9. _____
   A. y = −2   B. x = −2   C. x = 4   D. y = 4

Graphing Unit Review 1 *(cont.)*

10. Find the equation of the line passing through $(6, -3)$ with slope of $\frac{1}{2}$.   10._____

   A. $y = -\frac{1}{2}x$ C. $y = \frac{1}{2}x + 6$

   B. $y = \frac{1}{2}x$ D. $y = \frac{1}{2}x - 6$

11. Find the equation of the line passing through $(3, -4)$ and $(-3, 5)$.   11._____

   A. $y = -\frac{3}{2}x + \frac{1}{2}$ C. $y = -\frac{1}{6}x - \frac{7}{2}$

   B. $y = -\frac{1}{6}x + \frac{7}{2}$ D. $y = -\frac{3}{2}x - \frac{17}{2}$

12. Find the equation of the line parallel to the graph $y = -3x + 1$ and   12._____
    passing through the point $(-2, -1)$.

   A. $y = -3x + 5$ C. $y = -3x + 2$
   B. $y = x + 1$ D. $y = -3x - 7$

13. Which of the following is the graph of $2x + 3y = 3$?   13._____

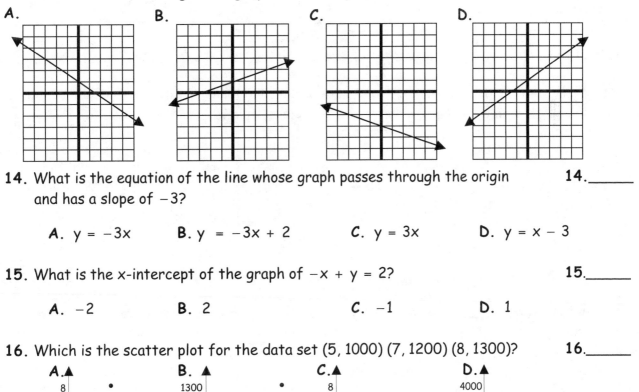

14. What is the equation of the line whose graph passes through the origin   14._____
    and has a slope of -3?

   A. $y = -3x$ B. $y = -3x + 2$ C. $y = 3x$ D. $y = x - 3$

15. What is the x-intercept of the graph of $-x + y = 2$?   15._____

   A. -2 B. 2 C. -1 D. 1

16. Which is the scatter plot for the data set $(5, 1000)$ $(7, 1200)$ $(8, 1300)$?   16._____

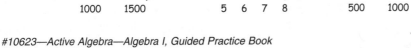

Name _____

Measurement Review (Graphing Unit)

1. Find the volume of the following shape. (Round to the nearest hundredth.)

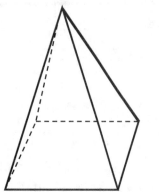

Side is 3.5 cm.
Height is 10.5 cm.

Volume = _____

2. Find the area of the following shape.

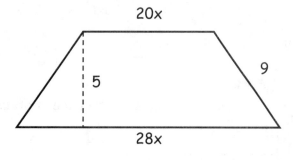

20x

5

9

28x

Area = _____

3. Mr. Wheat needed to make a stand for a project in his auto shop. He used a cinder block with a hole cut out of the center, as shown below.

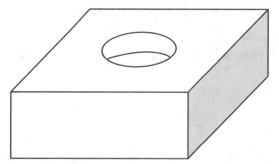

Which formula could be used to find the volume of the stand?

A. $V = lwh + \pi r^2 h$

B. $V = lwh$

C. $V = \pi r^2 h$

D. $V = lwh - \pi r^2 h$

Measurement Review (Graphing Unit) *(cont.)*

4. Find the volume of the following shape. (Exclude the volume of the holes.)

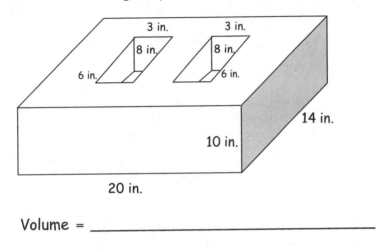

Volume = _____

5. Find the surface area of the following net of a square pyramid.

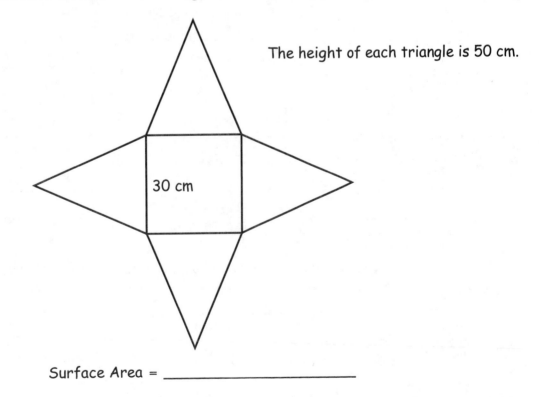

The height of each triangle is 50 cm.

30 cm

Surface Area = _____

Measurement Review (Graphing Unit) *(cont.)*

6. Find the area of the given figure.

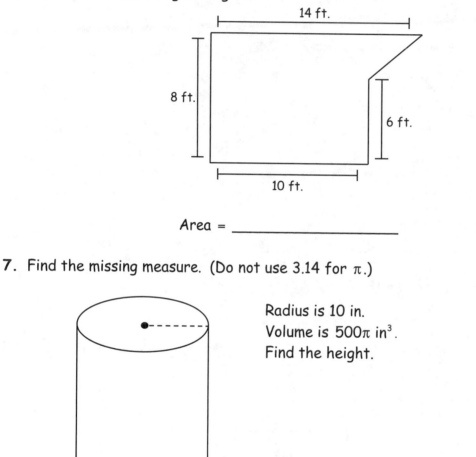

Area = _____

7. Find the missing measure. (Do not use 3.14 for π.)

Radius is 10 in.
Volume is 500π in³.
Find the height.

Height = _____

8. A cylindrical can of transmission fluid has a volume of 24 fluid ounces. A second cylindrical can has dimensions that are twice the size of the smaller can. Which is closest to the volume of the larger can?

A. 48 fl. oz.
B. 96 fl. oz.

C. 85 fl. oz.
D. 192 fl. oz.

Measurement Review (Graphing Unit) *(cont.)*

9. Find the missing measure. (Do not use 3.14 for π.)

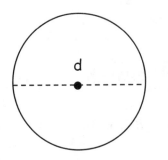

Area is 144π in^2.
Find the diameter.

Diameter = _____

10. Find the circumference of the following shape.

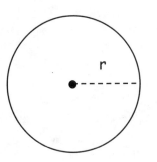

Diameter is 8 cm.

Circumference = _____

Name _____

Graphing Memorization Sheet

Graphing Memorization Sheet

$$m = \text{slope} = \frac{\text{rise}}{\text{run}}$$

positive slope (m) $\longrightarrow$ slants to the right

negative slope (m) $\longrightarrow$ slants to the left

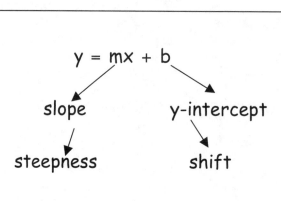

$y = mx + b$

slope   y-intercept

steepness   shift

$\dfrac{0}{2} = 0 \longrightarrow$ zero slope $\longrightarrow$ horizontal line

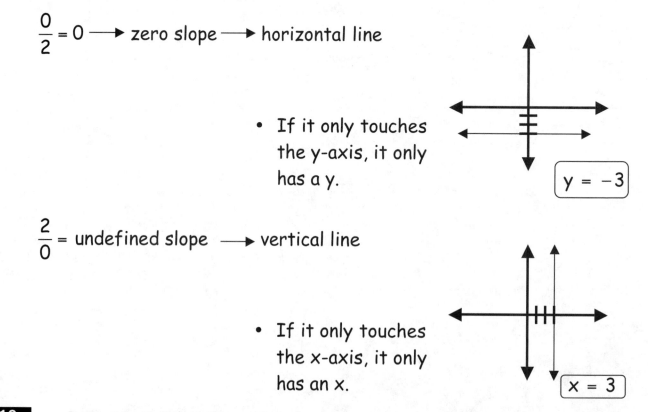

- If it only touches the y-axis, it only has a y.

$y = -3$

$\dfrac{2}{0} =$ undefined slope $\longrightarrow$ vertical line

- If it only touches the x-axis, it only has an x.

$x = 3$

Teacher Created Materials
PUBLISHING

#10623—Active Algebra—Algebra I, Guided Practice Book

Graphing Memorization Sheet *(cont.)*

To write the equation of a line, you need the following:
- 1 point (on the line)
- Slope (of the line)

Example:

$(3, 4)$ $m = -2$

Use: $y = mx + b$

or

$y - y_1 = m(x - x_1)$

If the problem refers to the x-intercept ⟶ DRAW A PICTURE.
(Find where the line crosses the x-axis.)

If the problem refers to the y-intercept ⟶ Write b = ____.
(The y-intercept is b.)

Name _____

Graphing Unit Review 2

Directions: Show your work neatly on another piece of paper.

1. Write the equation of the line passing through the points (3, 6) and (2, 6).   1._____
   A. $y = 3$ B. $y = 6$ C. $x = 2$ D. $y = 2$

2. Write the equation of the line passing through the points (−1, 4) and (−1, 5).   2._____
   A. $y = 4$ B. $y = -1$ C. $x = 2$ D. $x = -1$

3. Draw and label the line $y = -1$.

4. Draw and label the line $x = 3$.

5. What is the slope of the line passing through (4, −2) and (−3, 1)?   5._____
   A. $\dfrac{3}{7}$ B. $-\dfrac{1}{7}$ C. $\dfrac{1}{7}$ D. $-\dfrac{3}{7}$

6. Find the slope and the y-intercept of the line below.   6._____

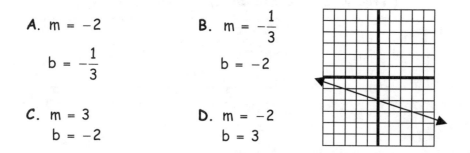

   A. $m = -2$ B. $m = -\dfrac{1}{3}$
      $b = -\dfrac{1}{3}$ $b = -2$

   C. $m = 3$ D. $m = -2$
      $b = -2$ $b = 3$

7. Find the equation of the line that passes through (−3, 1) with the slope of 0.   7._____
   A. $x = -3$ B. $x = -1$ C. $y = -1$ D. $y = 1$

8. What is the equation of the line whose graph has a slope of 2 and   8._____
   a y−intercept of −1?
   A. $y = 2x - 1$ C. $y = -2x + 1$
   B. $y = -x + 2$ D. $y = 2x + 1$

9. Find the equation of the line passing through (−2, 4) with an undefined slope.   9._____
   A. $y = -2$ B. $x = -2$ C. $x = 4$ D. $y = 4$

Graphing Unit Review 2 (cont.)

10. Find the equation of the line passing through $(4, -3)$ with slope of $\frac{2}{3}$.   10._____

    A. $y = \frac{2}{3}x + 6$ **C.** $y = \frac{2}{3}x - \frac{17}{3}$

    B. $y = \frac{2}{3}x - \frac{1}{3}$ **D.** $y = \frac{2}{3}x + 2$

11. Find the equation of the line passing through $(3, -4)$ and $(-3, 5)$.   11._____

    A. $y = -\frac{3}{2}x + \frac{1}{2}$ **C.** $y = -\frac{1}{6}x - \frac{7}{2}$

    B. $y = -\frac{1}{6}x + \frac{7}{2}$ **D.** $y = -\frac{3}{2}x - \frac{17}{2}$

12. Find the equation of the line parallel to the graph $y = 2x - 4$ and   12._____
passing through the point $(-4, 3)$.

    A. $y = -14x - 13$ **C.** $y = -4x + 19$

    B. $y = 2x - 5$ **D.** $y = 2x + 11$

13. Which of the following is the graph of $3y + x = -9$?   13._____

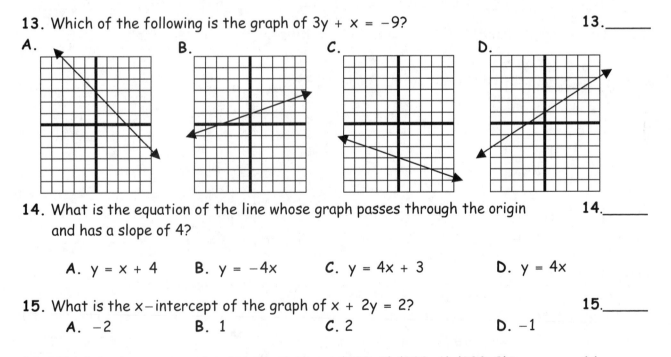

A.   **B.**   **C.**   **D.**

14. What is the equation of the line whose graph passes through the origin   14._____
and has a slope of 4?

    A. $y = x + 4$ **B.** $y = -4x$ **C.** $y = 4x + 3$ **D.** $y = 4x$

15. What is the x-intercept of the graph of $x + 2y = 2$?   15._____

    A. -2 **B.** 1 **C.** 2 **D.** -1

16. Which is the scatter plot for the data set $(500, 3)$ $(600, 6)$ $(800, 9)$?   16._____

Name _____

One-Variable Inequalities

Directions: Circle all correct solutions for each inequality.

1. $x > -4$ **A.** 5   **B.** 0   **C.** -4 **D.** -6

2. $y < 3$ **A.** 0   **B.** 3   **C.** -3 **D.** -1

3. $a \geq 4$ **A.** -4 **B.** 0   **C.** 4   **D.** 6

4. $m \leq 12$ **A.** 5   **B.** -12 **C.** 0   **D.** -13

5. $c < -3$ **A.** 0   **B.** -3 **C.** -4 **D.** 3

6. $a \geq 0$ **A.** 3   **B.** -2 **C.** 0   **D.** -1

Directions: Graph each of the following inequalities on the number line provided.

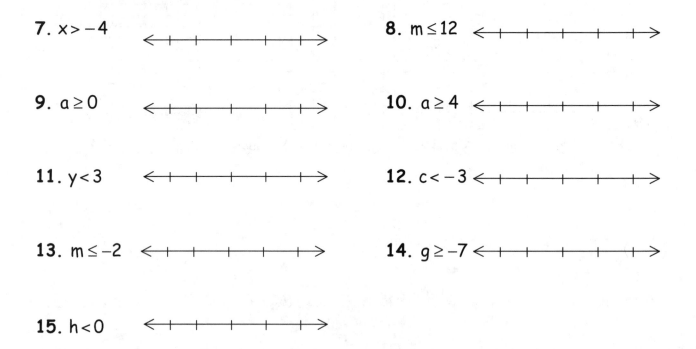

7. $x > -4$

8. $m \leq 12$

9. $a \geq 0$

10. $a \geq 4$

11. $y < 3$

12. $c < -3$

13. $m \leq -2$

14. $g \geq -7$

15. $h < 0$

Teacher Created Materials
PUBLISHING

#10623—Active Algebra—Algebra I, Guided Practice Book

One-Variable Inequalities (cont.)

Directions: Write the inequality shown by each graph.

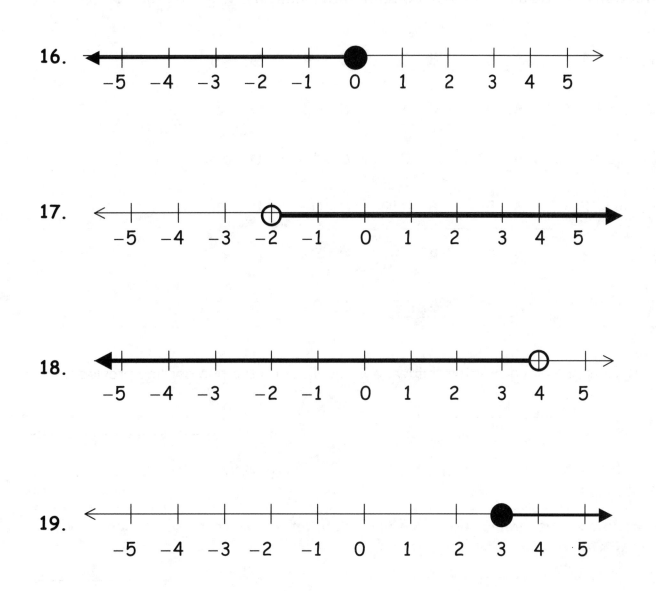

16.

17.

18.

19.

Name _____

Solving Compound Inequalities ("ands")

Directions: Graph each of the compound inequalities, and write the solution set.

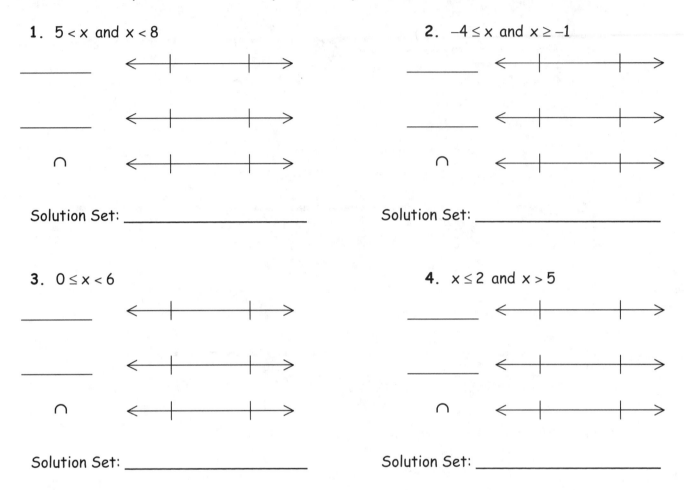

1. $5 < x$ and $x < 8$

_____

_____

$\cap$

Solution Set: _____

2. $-4 \leq x$ and $x \geq -1$

_____

_____

$\cap$

Solution Set: _____

3. $0 \leq x < 6$

_____

_____

$\cap$

Solution Set: _____

4. $x \leq 2$ and $x > 5$

_____

_____

$\cap$

Solution Set: _____

Directions: Solve, graph, and write the solution set for each compound inequality.

5. $4 < x + 6 < 7$

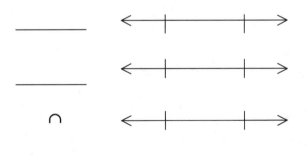

_____

_____

$\cap$

Solution Set: _____

6. $-25 \leq 5x \leq 20$

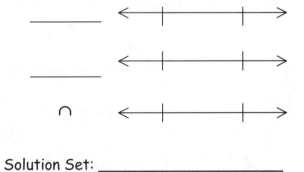

_____

_____

$\cap$

Solution Set: _____

Teacher Created Materials
PUBLISHING

#10623—*Active Algebra—Algebra I, Guided Practice Book*

Solving Compound Inequalities ("ands") (cont.)

7. $-9 \le 7x - 9 < 40$

8. $-3x - 6 > -6$ and $-3x - 6 > 9$

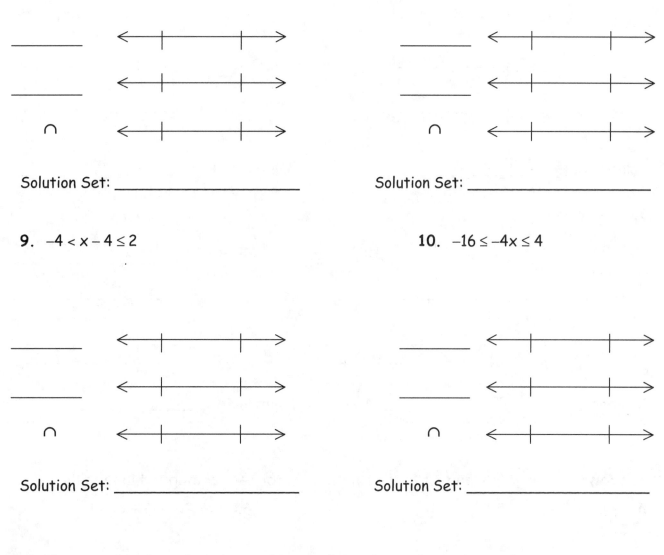

Solution Set: _____

Solution Set: _____

9. $-4 < x - 4 \le 2$

10. $-16 \le -4x \le 4$

Solution Set: _____

Solution Set: _____

Directions: Write the solution set of inequalities shown by each graph.

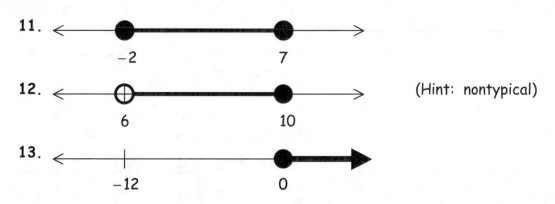

11.

-2 7

12.

6 10 (Hint: nontypical)

13.

-12 0

Teacher Created Materials
PUBLISHING

Name _____

Solving Compound Inequalities ("ors")

Directions: Graph each of the following compound inequalities, and write the solution set.

1. $x < 4$ or $x > 7$

_____ $\longleftrightarrow$

_____ $\longleftrightarrow$

$\cup$ $\longleftrightarrow$

Solution Set: _____

2. $-8 > x$ or $x < -2$

_____ $\longleftrightarrow$

_____ $\longleftrightarrow$

$\cup$ $\longleftrightarrow$

Solution Set: _____

3. $x > 1$ or $x \geq -3$

_____ $\longleftrightarrow$

_____ $\longleftrightarrow$

$\cup$ $\longleftrightarrow$

Solution Set: _____

4. $x > -2$ or $x \leq 4$

_____ $\longleftrightarrow$

_____ $\longleftrightarrow$

$\cup$ $\longleftrightarrow$

Solution Set: _____

Directions: Solve, graph, and write the solution set for each compound inequality.

5. $x + 9 < 6$ or $x - 5 > 3$

_____ $\longleftrightarrow$

_____ $\longleftrightarrow$

$\cup$ $\longleftrightarrow$

Solution Set: _____

6. $6x > 36$ or $4x \leq 16$

_____ $\longleftrightarrow$

_____ $\longleftrightarrow$

$\cup$ $\longleftrightarrow$

Solution Set: _____

Solving Compound Inequalities ("ors") *(cont.)*

7. $2x + 5 < 1$ or $4x - 7 \geq 9$

8. $x + 2 \leq 0$ or $x - 5 \geq 3$

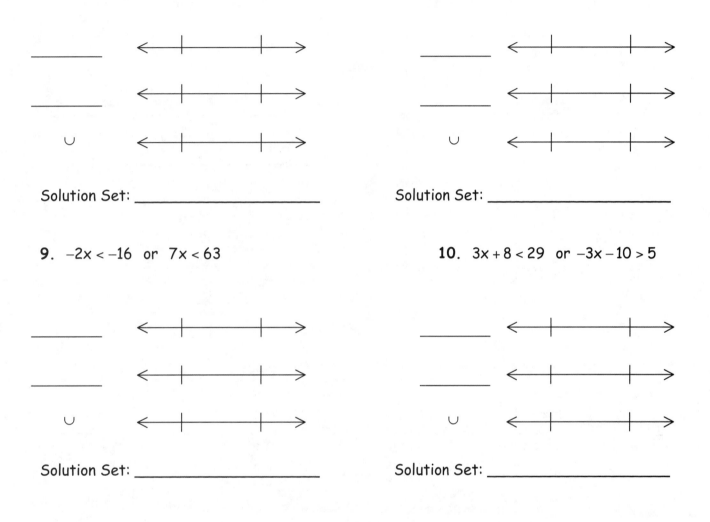

Solution Set: _____

Solution Set: _____

9. $-2x < -16$ or $7x < 63$

10. $3x + 8 < 29$ or $-3x - 10 > 5$

Solution Set: _____

Solution Set: _____

Directions: Write the solution set of inequalities shown by each graph.

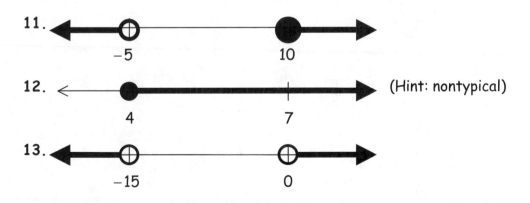

11. -5 10

12. 4 7 (Hint: nontypical)

13. -15 0

Teacher Created Materials
P U B L I S H I N G

Name _____

Compound Inequalities Review

Directions: Graph. Write the solution sets.

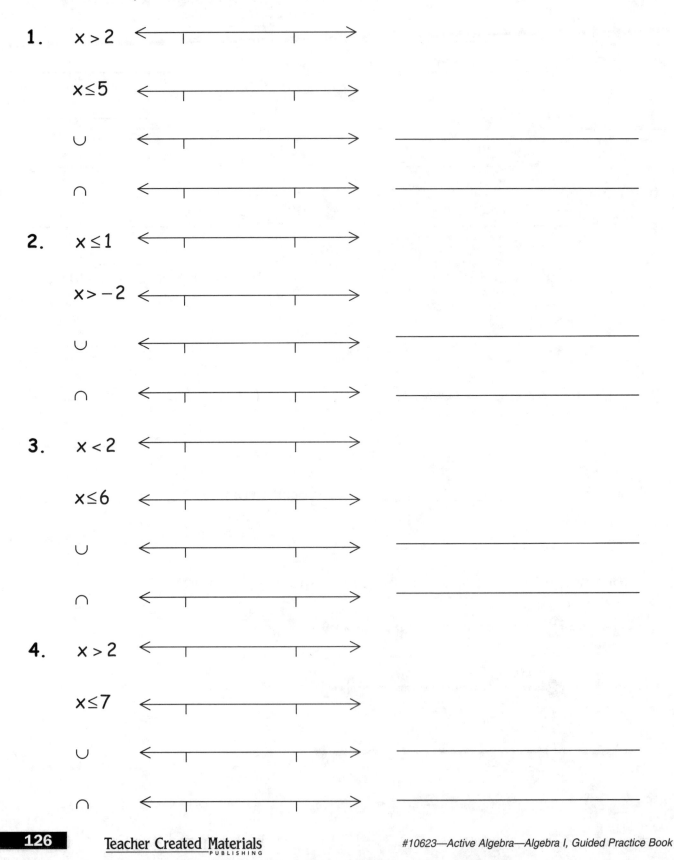

1. $x > 2$

$x \le 5$

$\cup$

$\cap$

2. $x \le 1$

$x > -2$

$\cup$

$\cap$

3. $x < 2$

$x \le 6$

$\cup$

$\cap$

4. $x > 2$

$x \le 7$

$\cup$

$\cap$

Compound Inequalities Review (cont.)

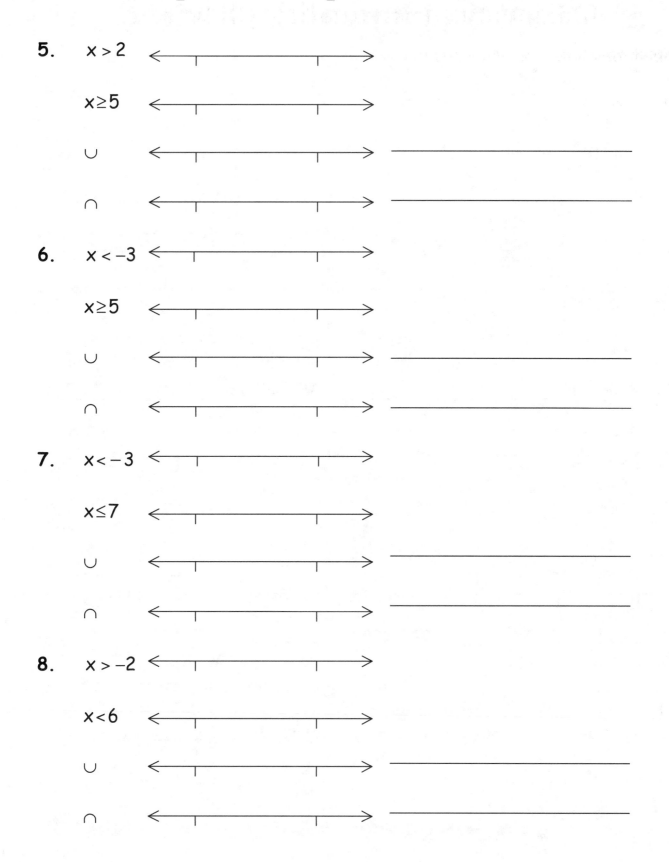

5. $x > 2$

   $x \geq 5$

   $\cup$

   $\cap$

6. $x < -3$

   $x \geq 5$

   $\cup$

   $\cap$

7. $x < -3$

   $x \leq 7$

   $\cup$

   $\cap$

8. $x > -2$

   $x < 6$

   $\cup$

   $\cap$

Name _____

Absolute Value Inequalities (Special Cases)

Directions: Solve each open sentence and graph.

1. $|x + 4| \geq 3$

_____ ⟵———+———+———⟶

_____ ⟵———+———+———⟶

_____ ⟵———+———+———⟶

Solution Set: _____

2. $|4x + 4| < 8$

_____ ⟵———+———+———⟶

_____ ⟵———+———+———⟶

_____ ⟵———+———+———⟶

Solution Set: _____

3. $|2x - 4| < 0$

_____ ⟵———+———+———⟶

_____ ⟵———+———+———⟶

_____ ⟵———+———+———⟶

Solution Set: _____

4. $|x + 3| > -2$

_____ ⟵———+———+———⟶

_____ ⟵———+———+———⟶

_____ ⟵———+———+———⟶

Solution Set: _____

Absolute Value Inequalities (Special Cases) *(cont.)*

5. $|x + 5| < -1$ **6.** $|x - 4| = -3$

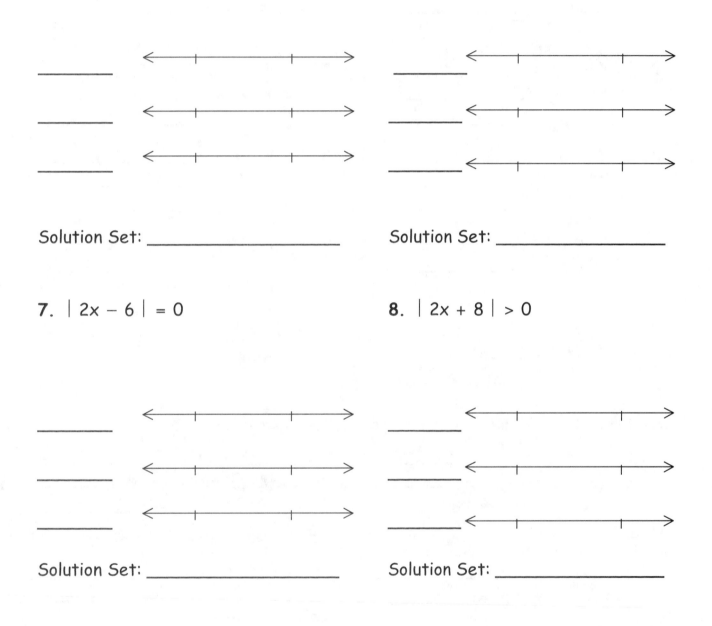

Solution Set: _____   Solution Set: _____

7. $|2x - 6| = 0$ **8.** $|2x + 8| > 0$

Solution Set: _____   Solution Set: _____

Name _____

Making Additive Inverses

Directions: Make additive inverses for the following.

1. (   )(6m) = _____
   (   )(8m) = _____
             = _____

6. (   )(−3x) = _____
   (   )(9x) = _____
             = _____

2. (   )(4n) = _____
   (   )(16n) = _____
             = _____

7. (   )(−6m) = _____
   (   )(−9m) = _____
             = _____

3. (   )(−4x) = _____
   (   )(5x) = _____
             = _____

8. (   )(−3x) = _____
   (   )(−3x) = _____
             = _____

4. (   )(10m) = _____
   (   )(6m) = _____
             = _____

9. (   )(−8x) = _____
   (   )(7x) = _____
             = _____

5. (   )(−5k) = _____
   (   )(−3k) = _____
             = _____

10. (   )(9f) = _____
   (   )(9f) = _____
             = _____

Directions: Make an additive inverse for each underlined variable.

11. (   )(4m + 5n) = _____
   (   )(−6m − 10n) = _____
             = _____

13. (   )(2k − 3m) = _____
   (   )(−5k − 4m) = _____
             = _____

12. (   )(2x + 3y) = _____
   (   )(5x − 4y) = _____
             = _____

14. (   )(4j + 3k) = _____
   (   )(5j + 3k) = _____
             = _____

Directions: Make additive inverses for either variable.

15. (   )(4x − 4y) = _____
   (   )(5x − 16y) = _____
             = _____

16. (   )(5k − 7f) = _____
   (   )(3k − 9f) = _____
             = _____

Name _____

Writing Systems of Equations 1

Directions: Assign two variables for each problem, and write the equations.
Do not solve.

1. A store receives a shipment of VCRs and CD players. A shipment of 5 VCRs and 4 CD players costs $1,950. A shipment of 3 VCRs and 6 CD players costs $2,250. Find the cost of a VCR and the cost of a CD player.

<u>Set up:</u>   <u>Equations:</u>

Let ____ = _____   _____

____ = _____   _____

2. A basketball team stopped at a fast-food restaurant after a game. They divided into two groups. One group bought 5 chicken sandwiches and 7 hamburgers for a cost of $24.90. The second group spent $28.80 and bought 5 chicken sandwiches and 9 hamburgers. How much does a hamburger cost?

<u>Set up:</u>   <u>Equations:</u>

Let ____ = _____   _____

____ = _____   _____

3. A travel agent offers 2 package vacation plans. The first plan costs $400 and includes 3 days at a hotel and a rental car for 2 days. The second plan costs $550 and includes 4 days at a hotel and a rental car for 3 days. The daily charge for the room and the car is the same under each plan. Find the cost per day for the room and for the car.

<u>Set up:</u>   <u>Equations:</u>

Let ____ = _____   _____

____ = _____   _____

Writing Systems of Equations 1 (cont.)

4. The Math Club is having their end-of-the-year party. Natasha found that the cafeteria usually makes 200 cups of pineapple-ginger ale fruit punch. The cook told her that if she doubles the pineapple and triples the ginger ale, she will have a total of 420 cups of punch. How many cups of each are needed to make 420 cups of fruit punch?

<u>Set up:</u>   <u>Equations:</u>

Let ____ = _____   _____

       ____ = _____   _____

5. A cruise ship has 680 rooms. Those with a view rent for $160 per night, and those without a view rent for $105 per night. On a night when the ship was completely occupied, revenues were $92,500. How many rooms of each type are on the ship?

<u>Set up:</u>   <u>Equations:</u>

Let ____ = _____   _____

       ____ = _____   _____

6. A pair of boots and a pair of tennis shoes cost $196.12. The difference in their cost is $44.38. Determine the cost of each type of footwear.

<u>Set up:</u>   <u>Equations:</u>

Let ____ = _____   _____

       ____ = _____   _____

Writing Systems of Equations 1 (cont.)

7. Two different types of batteries are needed to run Joshua's remote-controlled jeep. The two batteries produce a total voltage of 6.5 V. The difference in their voltage is 2.5 V. Determine the voltages of the two batteries.

<u>Set up:</u>   <u>Equations:</u>

Let ____ = _____   _____

____ = _____   _____

8. In the Alice High School band, the number of trumpet players is 4 times the number of French horn players. There are 35 trumpet and French horn players in the band. How many people play the trumpet?

<u>Set up:</u>   <u>Equations:</u>

Let ____ = _____   _____

____ = _____   _____

9. Jason, a vendor at the Minute Maid Park in Houston, sells two sizes of drinks. One costs $1.00 and the other costs $1.50. He knows he sold a total of 230 drinks for a total of $285.00. How many small drinks did he sell?

<u>Set up:</u>   <u>Equations:</u>

Let ____ = _____   _____

____ = _____   _____

Name _____

Writing Systems of Equations 2

Directions: Assign two variables for each problem, and write the equations.
Do not solve.

1. Al has a $12 gift certificate to Aqua-land. He can buy 3 fish and 1 frog, or he can buy 2 frogs. Find the cost of each type of animal.

   Set up: Equations:

   Let ____ = _____   _____

   ____ = _____   _____

2. An electric guitar costs $781 more than an acoustic guitar. If 13 electric guitars and 12 acoustic guitars were sold, revenues would be $72,628. Find the cost of each guitar.

   Set up: Equations:

   Let ____ = _____   _____

   ____ = _____   _____

3. On the PSJA North tennis team, there are 9 more boys than girls. If there is a total of 21 players, how many boys are on the team?

   Set up: Equations:

   Let ____ = _____   _____

   ____ = _____   _____

4. Tashika went to Frosty's and bought fruit slushies for .75 cents each and cones for $1 each. She spent a total of $12.75 and she bought 15 total items. How many fruit slushies did she buy?

   Set up: Equations:

   Let ____ = _____   _____

   ____ = _____   _____

5. The cost of "Star Wars" on DVD is 2 times that of the VHS version. If 1 DVD and 2 VHS tapes cost $23.85, find the cost of a DVD and the cost of a VHS tape.

   Set up: Equations:

   Let ____ = _____   _____

   ____ = _____   _____

Writing Systems of Equations 2 *(cont.)*

6. Mr. Lege's third-period class collected $60 more this week than they did last week for the homeless shelter. Altogether, they collected $340. How much did they collect last week?

<u>Set up:</u>   <u>Equations:</u>

Let _____ = _____   _____

_____ = _____   _____

7. The basketball team has 20 more players than the baseball team does. There are 100 players total. How many basketball players are there?

<u>Set up:</u>   <u>Equations:</u>

Let _____ = _____   _____

_____ = _____   _____

Directions: Assign two variables, and write the equations. **Solve**.

8. For a fund-raiser, a Boy Scout troop sold two sizes of popcorn boxes—small for $3 and large for $6. If 302 boxes were sold with a cash receipt of $1,803, how many large boxes were sold?

<u>Set up:</u>   <u>Equations:</u>

Let _____ = _____   _____

_____ = _____   _____

<u>SOLVE:</u>

Writing Systems of Equations 2 (cont.)

Directions: Assign two variables for each problem, and write the equations. **Solve**.

9. Together, 1 small package of gum and 1 large package of gum cost $1.10. If you bought 2 small packages of gum and 1 large package of gum, they would cost $1.45. How much did the large package of gum cost?

<u>Set up:</u>   <u>Equations:</u>

Let _____ = _____   _____

_____ = _____   _____

<u>SOLVE:</u>

10. The Key Club is selling T-shirts and key chains. Its members sold a total of 261 items. Twice as many T-shirts were sold as key chains. How many items of each type were sold?

<u>Set up:</u>   <u>Equations:</u>

Let _____ = _____   _____

_____ = _____   _____

<u>SOLVE:</u>

Name _____

Writing Systems of Equations 3

Directions: Assign two variables for each problem, and write the equations. **Do not solve.**

1. Ranger Shoe Company manufactures two types of shoes, athletic shoes and casual shoes. The cost of manufacturing 20 pairs of athletic shoes and 10 pairs of casual shoes is $750. If 25 pairs of athletic shoes and 20 pairs of casual shoes were manufactured, the cost would be $1,200. How much does it cost to manufacture each type of shoe?

<u>Set up:</u>   <u>Equations:</u>

Let ____ = _____   _____

____ = _____   _____

2. Julio has a $60 gift certificate from a local bookstore. He was planning to spend the entire amount by purchasing 2 hardback books and 6 paperback books. However, he purchased only 2 hardback books and 3 paperback books, and he still has $20.25 left on the gift certificate. Find the cost of a hardcover book and the cost of a paperback book.

<u>Set up:</u>   <u>Equations:</u>

Let ____ = _____   _____

____ = _____   _____

3. To raise funds, the band sells two sizes of cookie dough, one for $6 and another for $10. If 205 containers of cookie dough were sold with cash receipts of $1,710, how many containers of each size were sold?

<u>Set up:</u>   <u>Equations:</u>

Let ____ = _____   _____

____ = _____   _____

4. Lauren spends her allowance, $50 a month, on makeup and CDs. She spends $10 more a month on CDs than she does on makeup. How much money does she spend every month on each product?

<u>Set up:</u>   <u>Equations:</u>

Let ____ = _____   _____

____ = _____   _____

Writing Systems of Equations 3 *(cont.)*

Directions: Assign two variables for each problem and write the equations. **Solve**.

5. The cost of Renegade's new CD is 3 times the cost of its tape. If 2 CDs and 3 tapes cost $47.70, what is the cost of each?

<u>Set up:</u>   <u>Equations:</u>

Let _____ = _____   _____

_____ = _____   _____

6. A small container of popcorn sells for $0.75, and a large container of popcorn sells for $1.25. How many containers of each size were sold if a total of 210 containers were sold for $232.50?

<u>Set up:</u>   <u>Equations:</u>

Let _____ = _____   _____

_____ = _____   _____

Name _____

Systems of Equations Unit Review 1

Directions: Show your work neatly on another sheet of paper.

1. Graph the lines formed by the system.

   $2y = -3x + 4$
   $y = -x + 1$

2. Find the solution to the system in problem 1.

   2._____

Directions: Use the graph to answer questions 3–5.

3. The ordered pair (3, 6) is the solution of the system of equations represented by which lines?

   3._____

   A. p and n   **C.** r and n
   B. p and m   **D.** r and m

4. Suppose that line "n" and the equation $x + 3y = 21$ represent a system of equations. How many solutions does this system have?

   4._____

   A. infinitely many   **B.** none   **C.** one   **D.** two

5. Which pair of lines is the graph of the system of equations listed below?

   $-3x + 2y = -8$
   $2x + 5y = -20$

   5._____

   A. n and p   **B.** p and m   **C.** r and p   **D.** r and m

6. When using the substitution method to solve the system of equations below, which of these expressions should be substituted for "y" in the second equation?

   $2x + y = -7$
   $3x + 4y = -13$

   6._____

   A. $2x - 7$ **B.** $-\dfrac{3}{4}x - \dfrac{13}{4}$ **C.** $\dfrac{3}{4}x - \dfrac{13}{4}$ **D.** $-2x - 7$

7. When using the substitution method to solve the system of equations below, which of these expressions should be substituted for "x" in the second equation?

   $x + 2y = 0$
   $2x - 3y = -7$

   7._____

   A. $-\dfrac{x}{2}$ **B.** $-2y$ **C.** $\dfrac{3}{2}y - \dfrac{7}{2}$ **D.** $\dfrac{2}{3}x + \dfrac{7}{3}$

Systems of Equations Unit Review 1 *(cont.)*

8. The zoo charges $4 for every adult and $2 for every child. Today, the zoo had 272 people in attendance and collected a total of $664. If a = the number of adults and c = the number of children, which of the following would you use to find the number of $4 and $2 admission fees collected by the zoo today?

    8._____

    A. $a + 2c = 664$ B. $a + c = 664$ C. $a - 272 = 664$ D. $4a + 2c = 664$
         $4a + c = 272$ $4a + 2c = 272$ $c - 272 = 664$ $a + c = 272$

9. Use the elimination method to find the value of "y" in the following system of equations. $-x + y = 6$
                                $x + y = 10$

    9._____

    A. 2   B. 16   C. 8   D. 4

10. Use the elimination method to find the value of "y" in the following system of equations. $x - 3y = 10$
                                $x - 4y = 6$

    10._____

    A. 4   B. 16   C. $-\dfrac{16}{7}$ D. $\dfrac{16}{7}$

11. What is the value of "x" if the following system of equations is solved by elimination? $2x + 2y = -8$
                                $3x + 8y = -7$

    11._____

    A. 1   B. 5   C. -5 D. -1

12. To eliminate the variable "y" in the system of equations, the second equation must be multiplied by which number? $5x + 4y = -2$
                                     $3x + y = -8$

    12._____

    A. $\dfrac{1}{4}$ B. 4   C. -4 D. -5

13. In total, 2 shirts and 3 pairs of jeans cost $138. Also, 3 shirts and 2 pairs of jeans cost $132. Find the cost of a shirt.

    13._____

    A. $60   B. $24   C. $48   D. $30

14. A CD player costs twice the amount of a boom box. Altogether, 2 CD players and 3 boom boxes cost $490. Find the cost of the CD player.

    14._____

    A. $70   B. $80   C. $160   D. $140

15. Graph:

    $y \le 2x + 1$

    $y > \dfrac{1}{3}x$

16. Graph:

    $y < \dfrac{1}{2}x - 1$

    $y > -1$

Name _____

Measurement Review (Systems Unit)

Directions: Show your work neatly.

1. Find the formula for each of the following:
   A. Trapezoid

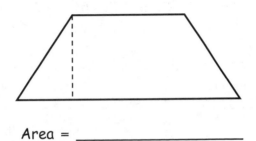

   Area = _____

   B. Rectangular prism

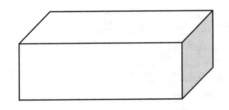

   Volume = _____

   C. Cube

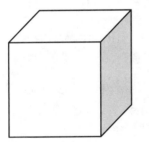

   Volume = _____

   Surface Area = _____

2. Find the area of the following shape.

The radius is 8 cm.

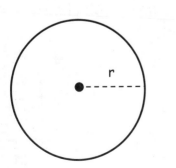

   Area = _____

Measurement Review (Systems Unit) *(cont.)*

3. Find the volume of the following shape. Round to the nearest cubic centimeter.

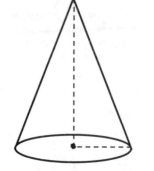

Height is 28 cm.
Radius is 5.8 cm.

Volume = _____

4. Which formula can be used to find the volume of the following composite solid?

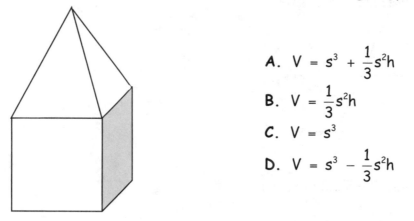

A. $V = s^3 + \dfrac{1}{3}s^2h$

B. $V = \dfrac{1}{3}s^2h$

C. $V = s^3$

D. $V = s^3 - \dfrac{1}{3}s^2h$

5. Ashley needed to make a stand for her history presentation. She used a cinder block with a hole cut out of the center, as shown below.

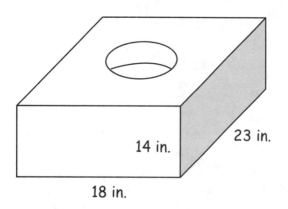

14 in.

23 in.

18 in.

The radius of the circle is 5 inches.
The height of the circle is 8 inches.

Find the volume of the stand.

Volume = _____

Measurement Review (Systems Unit) *(cont.)*

6. Find the surface area of the following net of a square pyramid.

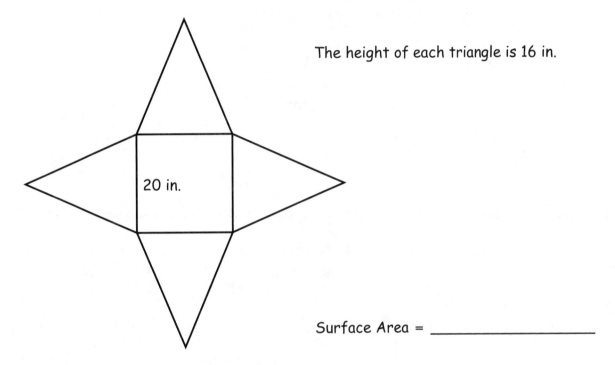

The height of each triangle is 16 in.

20 in.

Surface Area = _____

7. Find the area of the shaded region.

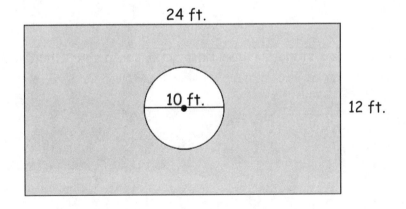

24 ft.

10 ft.

12 ft.

Area of Shaded Region = _____

Teacher Created Materials
PUBLISHING

Measurement Review (Systems Unit) *(cont.)*

8. Find the missing measure. (Do not use 3.14 for π.)

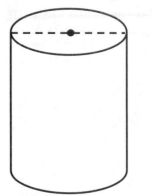

Diameter is 16 in.

Volume is 320π in.³

Find the height.

Height = _____

9. A box in the shape of a rectangular prism has a volume of 360 cubic inches. A second box has the dimensions that are half the size of the larger box. Find the volume of the smaller box.

Volume = _____

10. Find the area of the given figure.

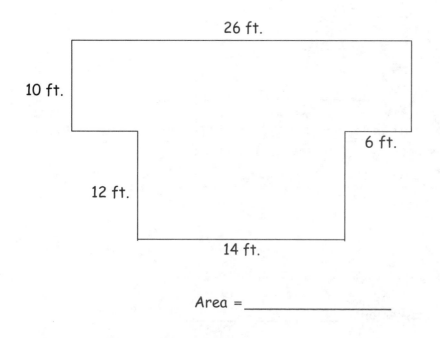

Area = _____

Name _____

Systems of Equations Unit Review 2

Directions: Show your work neatly on another sheet of paper.

1. Graph the lines formed by the system.
   $-2x + 3y = -6$
   $y = -2x + 6$

2. Find the solution to the system in problem 1.

2._____

Directions: Use the graph to answer questions 3–5.

3. The ordered pair $(0, -4)$ is the solution of the system of equations represented by lines

3._____

    A. p and n.   **C.** r and n.
    B. p and m.   **D.** r and m.

4. Suppose that line "n" and the equation $x + 3y = -12$ represent a system of equations. How many solutions does this system have?

4._____

    A. infinitely many   **B.** none   **C.** one   **D.** two

5. Which pair of lines is the graph of the following system of equations?
   $$-3x + 2y = -8$$
   $$x + 3y = 21$$

5._____

    A. n and p   **B.** n and m   **C.** r and p   **D.** r and m

6. When using the substitution method to solve the system of equations below, which of these expressions should be substituted for "y" in the second equation?
   $$-3x + y = 8$$
   $$4x - 2y = -10$$

6._____

    A. $-3x + 8$ **B.** $5x$ **C.** $2x + 5$ **D.** $3x + 8$

7. When using the substitution method to solve the system of equations below which of these expressions should be substituted for "x" in the second equation?
   $$x - 4y = -14$$
   $$4x - 3y = -17$$

7._____

    A. $-4y - 14$ **B.** $4y - 14$ **C.** $-18y$ **D.** $\frac{3}{4}y - \frac{17}{4}$

Systems of Equations Unit Review 2 *(cont.)*

8. Central High School's drama department performed a play. They charged $3   8._____
   for students and $6 for adults. There were 204 people in attendance with
   total receipts of $864 for the night. If a = the number of adults and s = the
   number of students, which of the following would you use to find the number
   of $3 and $6 admission fees collected for the performance?

   A. $6a + s = 864$ B. $a + s = 864$ C. $a - 204 = s$ D. $a + s = 204$
   $\quad\;\; a + 3s = 204$ $\quad 6a + 3s = 204$ $\quad s - 864 = a$ $\quad 6a + 3s = 864$

9. Use the elimination method to find the value of "y" in the following system   9._____
   of equations. $-x + 2y = 6$
   $\qquad\qquad\qquad\qquad\qquad\quad x + 3y = 4$

   A. 2   B. $\dfrac{2}{5}$ C. $\dfrac{5}{3}$ D. 10

10. Use the elimination method to find the value of "x" in the following   10._____
    system of equations. $x + 2y = 8$
    $\qquad\qquad\qquad\qquad\qquad\; x - 5y = -6$

    A. $\dfrac{2}{7}$ B. 4   C. $-\dfrac{2}{3}$ D. 2

11. If the following system of equations is solved by elimination, what is   11._____
    the value of "y"? $2x + 3y = 8$
    $\qquad\qquad\qquad\qquad\quad 3x - 6y = 12$

    A. 0   B. 4   C. $\dfrac{20}{7}$ D. $\dfrac{4}{7}$

12. To eliminate the variable "y" in the following system of equations,   12._____
    the second equation must be multiplied by which number?
    $\qquad\qquad\qquad\qquad 4x - 3y = -2$
    $\qquad\qquad\qquad\qquad 2x + y = -6$

    A. -2 B. -3 C. 2   D. 3

13. The cost of a new CD is 4 more than $\frac{1}{2}$ the cost of a DVD movie.   13._____
    If 2 CDs and 3 DVD movies cost $104, find the cost of 1 CD.
    A. $16   B. $24   C. $25   D. $16.50

14. In total, 2 baseballs and 3 footballs cost $67. A football is $4 more   14._____
    than 3 times the cost of a baseball. Find the cost of a baseball.
    A. $6   B. $7   C. $5   D. $4

15. Graph:
    $y \le 2x + 1$

16. Graph:
    $y \le 2$

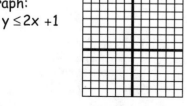

Teacher Created Materials
PUBLISHING

Name _____

Semester Review 1 (Graphing)

Directions: Show your work neatly on another sheet of paper.

1. Name the quadrant in which the ordered pair (−1, 2) is located.

   _____

Directions: Use the graph to answer questions 2–4.

2. State the relation shown in the graph.

   _____

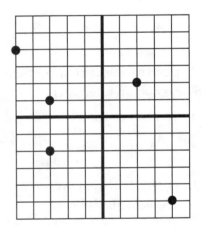

3. What is the domain of the relation shown in the graph?

   _____

4. What is the range of the relation shown in the graph?

   _____

5. What are the domain and range of the relation shown in the table below?

   5._____

x	y
2	3
4	5

   A. D = {2, 3}   R = {4, 5}   **C.** D = {2, 5}   R = {3, 4}
   B. D = {2, 4}   R = {3, 5}   **D.** D = {3, 2}   R = {5, 4}

6. What is the graph of the set of ordered pairs (a, 0), where "a" is any number?

   6._____

   A. the x-axis   **C.** the origin
   B. the y-axis   **D.** cannot be determined

Semester Review 1 (Graphing) *(cont.)*

7. Solve the equation $3a + 4m = 6$ for "m."

    A. $m = \dfrac{3}{4}a + \dfrac{3}{2}$

    B. $m = -\dfrac{3}{4}a - \dfrac{3}{2}$

    C. $m = -\dfrac{3}{4}a + \dfrac{3}{2}$

    D. $m = \dfrac{9a}{4}$

7._____

8. What is the range of the solution set of the equation $2c + 4d = 8$ if the domain is $\{-2, 0, 2\}$?

8._____

    A. $\{4, 6, 8\}$ **B.** $\{1, 2, 3\}$ **C.** $\{-1, -2, -3\}$ **D.** $\{0, 4, 8\}$

9. What is the domain of the solution set of the equation $3r - 6s = 6$ if the range is $\{-3, 0, 3\}$?

9._____

    A. $\{-8, -2, 4\}$ **B.** $\{-\dfrac{5}{2}, -1, \dfrac{1}{2}\}$ **C.** $\{-4, 2, 8\}$ **D.** $\{-3, 0, 3\}$

10. Which equation is a linear equation?

10._____

    A. $y = x^3$ **C.** $y = 2x + 3$

    B. $y = \dfrac{1}{x}$ **D.** $x^2 + y^2 = 9$

11. Determine which relation is a function?

11._____

    A.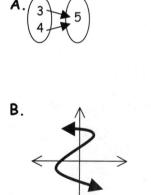

    C.

x	y
2	3
4	3
4	5

    B.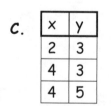

    D. $\{(3, 2), (3, 5)\}$

Semester Review 1 (Graphing) *(cont.)*

12. If $g(x) = 3x^2 - 4x$, what is the value of $g(-1)$?

    A. 1   **B.** 5   **C.** -7 **D.** 7   12._____

13. Which equation represents the function?

    A. $y = x + 6$ **C.** $y = 2x - 4$

    B. $y = 2x + 4$ **D.** $y = 3x + 4$ 13._____

x	1	3	5	7	9
y	6	10	14	18	22

14. Which equation represents the function?

    A. $y = \dfrac{1}{3}x - 2$ **C.** $y = 3x + 2$

    B. $y = 3x - 2$ **D.** $y = -\dfrac{1}{3}x - 2$ 14._____

x	0	3	6	9	12
y	-2	-3	-4	-5	-6

Name _____

Semester Review 2
(Writing One-Variable Equations)

Directions: Using one variable, write equations for the following. **Do not solve**.

1. The length of a rectangular field is 15 feet less than 4 times the width. The perimeter is 270 feet. Find the length.

   Let_____ = _____

   _____ = _____

   Equation: _____

2. The larger of two numbers is 10 less than 5 times the smaller. Their sum is 146. Find the larger number.

   Let_____ = _____

   _____ = _____

   Equation: _____

3. Together, a football and a basketball cost $65. A football costs $5 more than $\frac{1}{2}$ of what a basketball costs. How much does a football cost?

   Let_____ = _____

   _____ = _____

   Equation: _____

4. The sum of three numbers is 75. The second number is 5 more than 4 times the first number, and the third number is 2 times the first. Find the second number.

   Let_____ = _____

   _____ = _____

   _____ = _____

   Equation: _____

Semester Review 2
(Writing One-Variable Equations) *(cont.)*

Directions: Using one variable, write equations for the following. **Do not solve.**

5. If 7 less than 4 times a number is 29, find the number.

Let_____ = _____

Equation: _____

Directions: Using one variable, write equations for the following. **Solve.**

6. Carlos and Mark went running. Carlos ran 2 miles less than half as many miles as Mark ran. Carlos ran 6 miles. How many miles did Mark run?

Let_____ = _____   Solve:

_____ = _____

Equation: _____

7. Together, a bat, a glove, and a uniform cost $285. The bat costs $5 more than twice the cost of the uniform, and the glove costs $20 more than the uniform. How much does the glove cost?

Let_____ = _____   Solve:

_____ = _____

_____ = _____

Equation: _____

8. Mrs. Edgar cut a piece of wire that was 125 cm long into two pieces. The first piece was 10 cm less than 4 times the second piece. Find the length of both pieces of wire.

Let_____ = _____   Solve:

_____ = _____

Equation: _____

Name _____

Semester Review 3 (Mixed Objectives)

1. Kara has the choice of 3 different vegetables on a menu. She then has the choice of 4 different entrées from the menu. How many food combinations exist if she chooses 1 vegetable and 1 entrée?

   A. 7   **B.** 12   **C.** 1   **D.** 16

   1._____

2. On Tuesday, Just Deals received a shipment of 240 Christmas trees. The manager had ordered 300 trees. What percent of her order arrived on Tuesday?

   A. 24%   **B.** 30%   **C.** 80%   **D.** 20%

   2._____

3. The Nguyens insured their house for $78,400, which is 80% of the total value of the house. What is the value of their house?

   <u>Proportion</u>   <u>Solve</u>

4. A stereo, sold at a discount of 25%, was purchased for $187.50. What was the price of the stereo before the discount?

   <u>Proportion</u>   <u>Solve</u>

5. Eli scored 85% on a test, and 6 problems were wrong. How many problems were on the test?

   <u>Proportion</u>   <u>Solve</u>

Semester Review 3 (Mixed Objectives) *(cont.)*

6. René received a commission of 6% on the sale of a new house. If the amount of his commission was $6,300, what was the selling price of the house?

<u>Proportion</u>   <u>Solve</u>

7. If the digits can be repeated, how many 4-digit numbers can be formed using the digits 8, 3, 5, and 2?

    A. 64   **B.** 24   **C.** 32   **D.** 256

7._____

8. How many ways can 4 people be arranged in a row?

    A. 256   **B.** 32   **C.** 64   **D.** 24

8._____

9. If the digits cannot be repeated, how many 3-digit numbers can be formed using only the digits 3, 8, 4, and 2?

    A. 64   **B.** 24   **C.** 256   **D.** 32

9._____

10. A die and a coin are tossed. What is the probability of tossing a 5 and heads?

    A. $\frac{1}{4}$ **B.** $\frac{1}{8}$ **C.** $\frac{1}{12}$ **D.** $\frac{1}{6}$

10._____

11. If four coins are tossed, what is the probability of tossing all heads?

    A. $\frac{1}{2}$ **B.** $\frac{1}{16}$ **C.** $\frac{1}{4}$ **D.** $\frac{1}{8}$

11._____

12. Jamie can make 12 bows every hour. Which proportion will give the number of bows Jamie can make in 20 hours?

    A. $\frac{12}{1}=\frac{x}{20}$ **B.** $\frac{12}{1}=\frac{20}{x}$ **C.** $\frac{12}{20}=\frac{1}{x}$ **D.** $\frac{20}{12}=\frac{x}{1}$

12._____

Name _____

Semester Review 4 (Graphing)

Directions: Show your work neatly on another sheet of paper.

1. Write the equation of the line passing through the points (2, 2) and (2, 5).   1._____

    A. y = 2   **B.** y = 3   **C.** x = 2   **D.** y = 5

2. Write the equation of the line passing through the points (−1, 4) and (2, 4).   2._____

    A. y = 4   **B.** y = −1   **C.** x = 2   **D.** x = −1

3. Draw and label the line x = 3.   4. Draw and label the line y = −2.

5. What is the slope of the line passing through (−2, 3) and (−3, 1)?   5._____

    A. $-\dfrac{2}{5}$ **B.** −2   **C.** $\dfrac{2}{5}$ **D.** 2

6. Find the slope and the y-intercept of the line below.   6._____

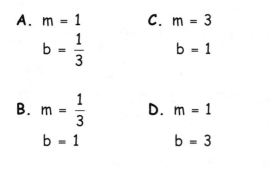

    A. m = 1   **C.** m = 3

         b = $\dfrac{1}{3}$ b = 1

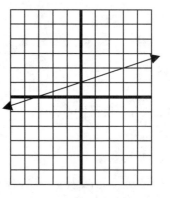

    B. m = $\dfrac{1}{3}$ **D.** m = 1

         b = 1   b = 3

7. What is the equation of the line whose graph has a slope of −3 and   7._____
a y-intercept of 2?

    A. y = −3x + 2   **C.** y = −2x + 1
    B. y = 2x − 3   **D.** y = 3x − 2

Semester Review 4 (Graphing) *(cont.)*

8. Find the equation of the line going through the point (6, −3) with a
slope of $\frac{1}{2}$.

   8._____

   A. $y = -\frac{1}{2}x$ **C.** $y = \frac{1}{2}x + 6$

   B. $y = \frac{1}{2}x$ **D.** $y = \frac{1}{2}x - 6$

9. Find the equation of the line parallel to the graph $y = -3x + 1$ and
passing through the point (−2, −1).

   9._____

   A. $y = -3x + 5$ **C.** $y = -3x - 7$
   B. $y = x + 1$ **D.** $y = -3x + 2$

10. Which of the following is the graph of $2x + 3y = 3$?

    10._____

    A.   **B.**   **C.**   **D.**

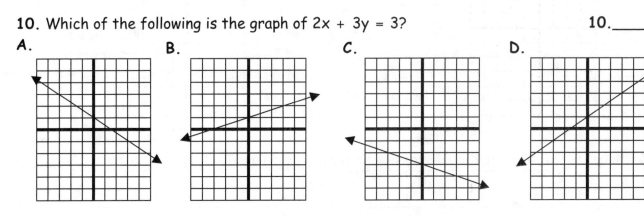

11. What is the equation of the line whose graph passes through the origin
and has a slope of −3?

    11._____

    A. $y = -3x$ **B.** $y + 3x = 2$ **C.** $y - 3x = 0$ **D.** $y = x - 3$

12. Which is the scatter plot for the data set (5, 1,000), (7, 1,200), (8, 1,300)?   12._____

    A.   **B.**   **C.**   **D.**

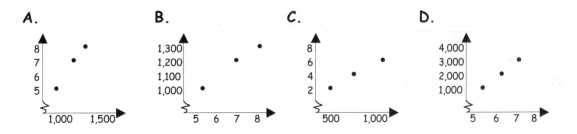

Name _____

Semester Review 5
(Writing Two-Variable Equations)

Directions: Assign two variables for each problem, and write the equations.
Do not solve.

1. A store receives a shipment of bicycles and scooters. A shipment of 5 bicycles
   and 4 scooters costs $1,950. A shipment of 3 bicycles and 6 scooters costs $2,250.
   Find the cost of a bicycle and the cost of a scooter.

   <u>Set up:</u>   <u>Equations:</u>

   Let ____ = _____   _____

   ____ = _____   _____

2. A youth group stopped at a fast-food restaurant after a game. They divided into two
   groups. One group bought 5 chicken sandwiches and 7 orders of fries for a cost of
   $24.90. The second group spent $28.80 and bought 5 chicken sandwiches and
   9 orders of fries. How much does an order of fries cost?

   <u>Set up:</u>   <u>Equations:</u>

   Let ____ = _____   _____

   ____ = _____   _____

3. A travel agent offers 2 package vacation plans. The first plan costs $400 and
   includes 3 days at a hotel and a rental car for 4 days. The second plan costs $550
   and includes 4 days at a hotel and a rental car for 5 days. The daily charge for the
   room and the car is the same under each plan. Find the cost per day for the room
   and for the car.

   <u>Set up:</u>   <u>Equations:</u>

   Let ____ = _____   _____

   ____ = _____   _____

4. Anton made 4 less than half the points that Jaron made at the basketball game last
   night. Together, they made 41 points. How many points did Anton make?

   <u>Set up:</u>   <u>Equations:</u>

   Let ____ = _____   _____

   ____ = _____   _____

Semester Review 5
(Writing Two-Variable Equations) (cont.)

Directions: Assign two variables for each problem, and write the equations. **Solve**.

5. A hotel has 680 rooms. Those with a view rent for $160 per night, and those without a view rent for $105 per night. On a night when the hotel was completely occupied, revenues were $100,000. How many rooms of each type are in the hotel?

Set up:

Let ____ = _____

____ = _____

Equations:

_____

_____

Solve:

6. In the Edcouch-Elsa High School band, the number of clarinet players is 4 times as many as the number of trombone players. There are 35 clarinet and trombone players in the band. How many people play the clarinet and how many play the trombone?

Set up:

Let ____ = _____

____ = _____

Equations:

_____

_____

Solve:

Name _____

Adding and Multiplying Monomials 1

Directions: Simplify.

1. $2x + 3x$ = _____

2. $-5m + 6m$ = _____

3. $-4y - 7y$ = _____

4. $-5a + 6a - 3a$ = _____

5. $2x - 3y + 4x - 6y$ = _____

6. $-3x + 4y + 3x - 5y$ = _____

7. $3a^2b - 2ab^2 - 5a^2b$ = _____

8. $-6mn + 4mn - 3m$ = _____

9. $3x(4x^2)$ = _____

10. $-2m(3m)$ = _____

11. $-6k(4y)$ = _____

12. $-2a(-3x^2)$ = _____

13. $-6(3x - 4)$ = _____

14. $-3x(2x^2 - 5y)$ = _____

15. $-2m(3m^3 - 4m^2)$ = _____

16. $-2xy^3(3xy^5)$ = _____

17. $-5y - 8y$ = _____

18. $6k(-2y)$ = _____

19. $3m^2n(6mn)$ = _____

20. $-5(2x - 6)$ = _____

21. $-6m + 4m - 2m^2$ = _____

22. $-2x + 5y - 6x + 4y$ = _____

23. $-5m^2(3m^3n + 4m)$ = _____

24. $2m^3(-5mn)$ = _____

25. $-6xy^2 - 5xy + 6xy^2$ = _____

26. $-3x + 4 - 6x(2x - 3) + 4(2x - 3) + x$ = _____

Name _____

Adding and Multiplying Monomials 2

Directions: Simplify.

1. $12x + 3x =$ _____

2. $6p - 8p =$ _____

3. $-4k - 6k =$ _____

4. $-3m + 6m - 4m =$ _____

5. $3p - 6x - 5p + 4x =$ _____

6. $-6m + 8n + 6m - 10m =$ ____

7. $-4x^2y - 6xy^2 + 3x^2y =$ _____

8. $-3ab - 6ab + 5b =$ _____

9. $4m(2m^2) =$ _____

10. $-6p(-3p^3) =$ _____

11. $-6x(3y) =$ _____

12. $-6a(4x^2) =$ _____

13. $-3(2x + 4) =$ _____

14. $-6p(3p^2 - 6p) =$ _____

15. $-5x(3x + 4) =$ _____

16. $-3xy^3(2x^2y^5) =$ _____

17. $-6y + 3y =$ _____

18. $-8y(2y^3) =$ _____

19. $4m^2n(3mn^2) =$ _____

20. $-3(2x - 6) =$ _____

21. $-8p + 4 - 6p =$ _____

22. $-p + 5n - 6p + 3n =$ _____

23. $-6p^2(3p^2 - 6n) =$ _____

24. $5x^2(3xy^2) =$ _____

25. $-6pm^2 - 4p^2m - 8pm^2 =$ _____

26. $-3p - 4p(3p - 5) - 6p(2p + 1) =$ _____

Teacher Created Materials
PUBLISHING

Name _____

Adding Polynomials Using Algebra Tiles

Directions: Use algebra tiles to simplify.

1. $(3x^2 + 2x - 1) + (-x^2 - 3x - 2) =$ _____

2. $(x^2 - 3x - 1) + (-2x^2 - x + 1) =$ _____

3. $(x^2 - 4x - 2) - (x^2 - 3x + 3) =$ _____

4. $(2x^2 - 2x + 4) - (-x^2 + 2x + 3) =$ _____

5. $(2x^2 - x - 1) + (x^2 - 4x - 2) =$ _____

6. $(-x^2 - 6x - 1) - (2x^2 - 3x - 1) =$ _____

Name _____

Adding and Multiplying Monomials 3

Directions: Simplify.

1. $2x - 6x$ = _____

2. $3mn - 5mn$ = _____

3. $6p^2 - 10p^2$ = _____

4. $8xy - 10xy$ = _____

5. $-3m^2n - 6m^2n$ = _____

6. $-3x + 4y$ = _____

7. $-8m - m - 2m$ = _____

8. $4x - 6y - 10x$ = _____

9. $4x(-3x^2)$ = _____

10. $-10y(y^3)$ = _____

11. $4x(6y)$ = _____

12. $-3mn^2(-4m^2n)$ = _____

13. $-3p^2(4p - 6)$ = _____

14. $-8(3x - 2)$ = _____

15. $-6a(4a - 6a^2)$ = _____

16. $-6xy^2(3xy)$ = _____

17. $3mn - 10mn$ = _____

18. $4p(3p^2)$ = _____

19. $-6n - 10n^2 - 6n$ = _____

20. $-3x^2(4x - 6)$ = _____

21. $-5m - 6m + 10m$ = _____

22. $8x(6x^2)$ = _____

23. $4xy^2(3xy)$ = _____

24. $-6p + 8p$ = _____

25. $-6p(8p)$ = _____

26. $-3p - 6p(2p + 1) - 4p(3p - 5)$ = _____

Teacher Created Materials
PUBLISHING

Name _____

Perimeter of Triangles

Directions: Find the length of each missing side.

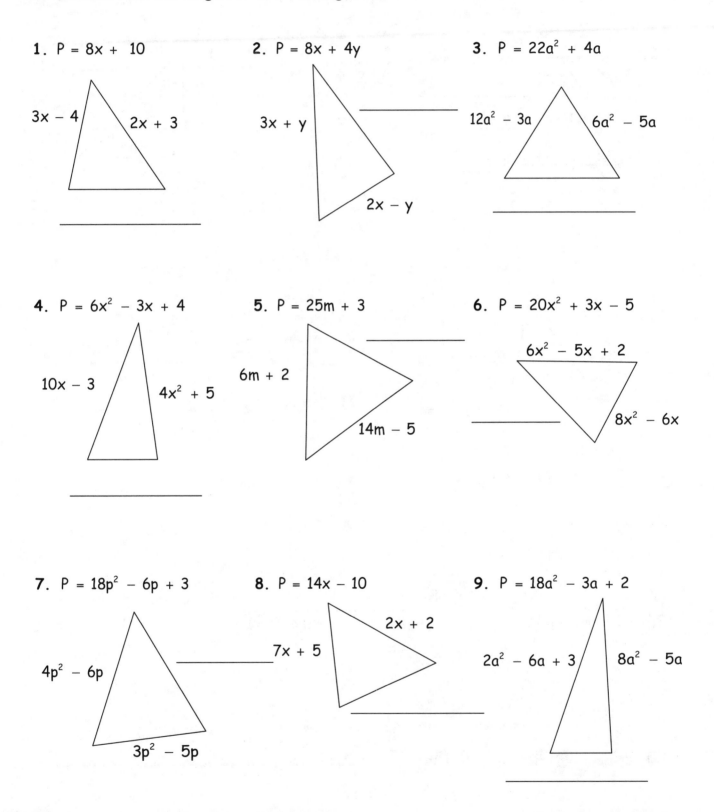

1. $P = 8x + 10$

$3x - 4$ $2x + 3$

_____

2. $P = 8x + 4y$

$3x + y$ _____

$2x - y$

3. $P = 22a^2 + 4a$

$12a^2 - 3a$ $6a^2 - 5a$

_____

4. $P = 6x^2 - 3x + 4$

$10x - 3$ $4x^2 + 5$

_____

5. $P = 25m + 3$

$6m + 2$ _____

$14m - 5$

6. $P = 20x^2 + 3x - 5$

$6x^2 - 5x + 2$

_____ $8x^2 - 6x$

7. $P = 18p^2 - 6p + 3$

$4p^2 - 6p$ _____

$3p^2 - 5p$

8. $P = 14x - 10$

$2x + 2$

$7x + 5$

_____

9. $P = 18a^2 - 3a + 2$

$2a^2 - 6a + 3$ $8a^2 - 5a$

_____

Name _____

Angle Measures

Directions: Find the measure of each missing angle.

1.

3x   2x – 10

2.

4x
2x – 7

_____

3.

4p
6p – 3

4.

m + 3
3m – 2

_____

5.

2x + 3   2x + 3

_____

6.

7x   8x – 3

_____

7.

4p
3p + 8

_____

8.

9x – 3   10x – 2

_____

9.

6a – 10
4a

_____

Teacher Created Materials
PUBLISHING

Name _____

Area and Perimeter

Directions: Find the area and perimeter of each rectangle.

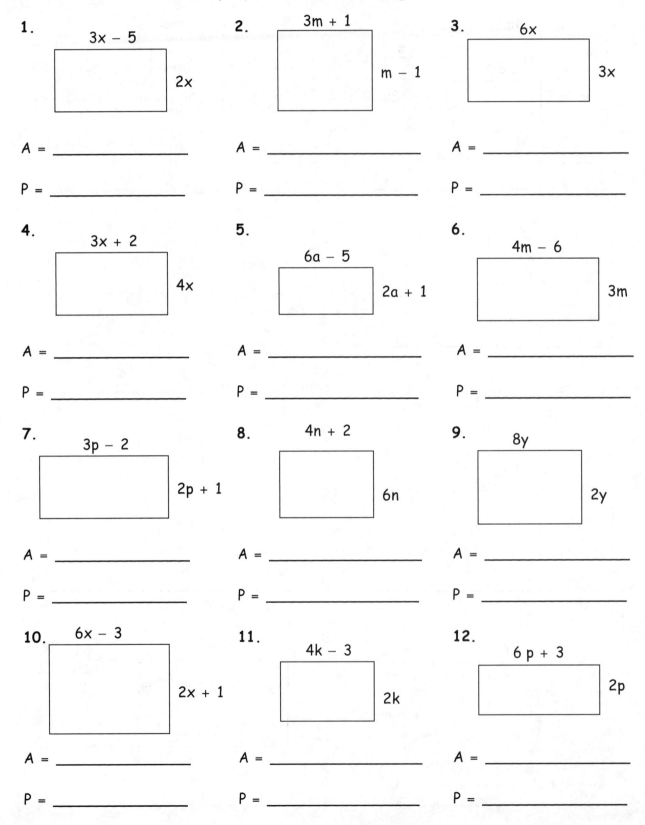

1.

3x − 5

2x

A = _____

P = _____

2.

3m + 1

m − 1

A = _____

P = _____

3.

6x

3x

A = _____

P = _____

4.

3x + 2

4x

A = _____

P = _____

5.

6a − 5

2a + 1

A = _____

P = _____

6.

4m − 6

3m

A = _____

P = _____

7.

3p − 2

2p + 1

A = _____

P = _____

8.

4n + 2

6n

A = _____

P = _____

9.

8y

2y

A = _____

P = _____

10.

6x − 3

2x + 1

A = _____

P = _____

11.

4k − 3

2k

A = _____

P = _____

12.

6 p + 3

2p

A = _____

P = _____

Name _____

Area of Shaded Region

Directions: Find the area of each shaded region in simplest terms.

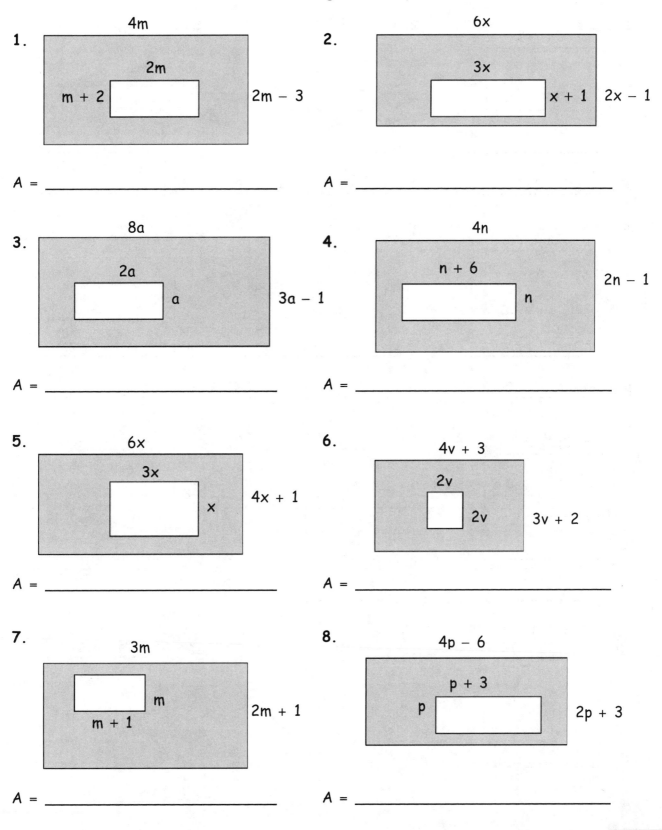

1.

4m

2m

m + 2

2m − 3

A = _____

2.

6x

3x

x + 1

2x − 1

A = _____

3.

8a

2a

a

3a − 1

A = _____

4.

4n

n + 6

n

2n − 1

A = _____

5.

6x

3x

x

4x + 1

A = _____

6.

4v + 3

2v

2v

3v + 2

A = _____

7.

3m

m

m + 1

2m + 1

A = _____

8.

4p − 6

p + 3

p

2p + 3

A = _____

Name _____

Geometry Review (Polynomials Unit)

Directions: Find the measure of the third side of each triangle.

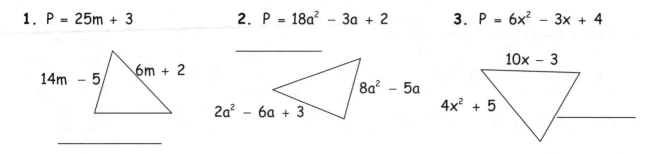

1. $P = 25m + 3$

14m − 5 / 6m + 2

_____

2. $P = 18a^2 − 3a + 2$

_____

$8a^2 − 5a$

$2a^2 − 6a + 3$

3. $P = 6x^2 − 3x + 4$

$10x − 3$

$4x^2 + 5$

_____

Directions: Find the measure of each missing angle.

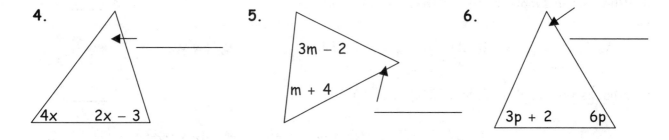

4.

4x   2x − 3

_____

5.

3m − 2

m + 4

_____

6.

_____

3p + 2   6p

Directions: Find the area of each shaded region in simplest terms.

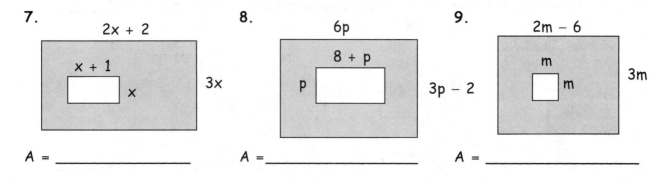

7.

2x + 2

x + 1

x   3x

A = _____

8.

6p

8 + p

p   3p − 2

A = _____

9.

2m − 6

m

m   3m

A = _____

Directions: Find the area and perimeter of each rectangle.

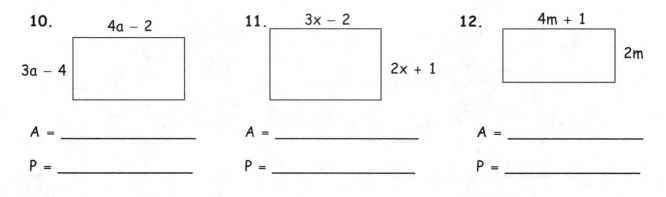

10.

4a − 2

3a − 4

A = _____

P = _____

11.

3x − 2

2x + 1

A = _____

P = _____

12.

4m + 1

2m

A = _____

P = _____

Name _____

Polynomials Unit Review 1

Directions: Show your work neatly on another piece of paper.

1. What is the simplest form of $m^3 \cdot m^2$?　　　　　　　　　　　1._____

    A. m^6　　　　　**B.** $2m^5$　　　　　**C.** $2m^6$　　　　　**D.** m^5

2. What is the simplest form of $(-2a^2b)(-7ab^3)$?　　　　　2._____

    A. $14a^2b^3$　　　**B.** $-14a^3b^4$　　　**C.** $-9a^2b^3$　　　**D.** $14a^3b^4$

3. What is the simplest form of $(3xy^3)(2xy)^3$?　　　　　　3._____

    A. $9xy^3$　　　　**B.** $24x^4y^6$　　　**C.** $24xy^3$　　　**D.** $6x^4y^4$

4. What is the simplest form of $(2x)^2 + (3x^2)^2$?　　　　　4._____

    A. $13x^6$　　　**B.** $4x^2 + 9x^4$　　**C.** $13x^5$　　**D.** $4x + 9x^2$

5. What is the simplest form of $\dfrac{4p^3n}{16p^5n}$? (Assume that the denominator is　　5._____

    not equal to zero.)

    A. $\dfrac{1}{4p^8}$　　　**B.** $4p^2$　　　**C.** $\dfrac{1}{12p^2}$　　　**D.** $\dfrac{1}{4p^2}$

6. What is the simplest form of $\dfrac{2x^{-3}y}{6xy^{-2}}$? (Assume that the denominator is　　6._____

    not equal to zero.)

    A. $\dfrac{y^3}{4x^4}$　　　**B.** $\dfrac{y^3}{2x^4}$　　　**C.** $\dfrac{y^3}{3x^4}$　　　**D.** $\dfrac{y^2}{3x^3}$

7. What is 420,000 expressed in scientific notation?　　　　7._____

    A. 4.2×10^5　　**B.** 42×10^4　　**C.** 4.2×10^{-5}　　**D.** 42×10^{-4}

Polynomials Unit Review 1 *(cont.)*

8. What is the value of $(2 \times 10^5)(3 \times 10^5)$?　　　　　　　8._____

　　A. 5×10^8　　　　B. 6×10^{10}　　　　C. 6×10^2　　　　D. 6×10^{15}

9. What is the simplest form of $-6(2x)^3(4x^2)$?　　　　　　9._____

　　A. $-192x^5$　　　　B. $-192x^2$　　　　C. $-48x^5$　　　　D. $4x^5$

10. What is the simplest form of $(3p^2 - 4p + 1) + (2p^2 + 4p - 5)$?　　10._____

　　A. $6p^2 - 4$　　　　　　　　　C. $5p^2 - 4$

　　B. $5p^4 - 4$　　　　　　　　　D. $5p^2 - 8p - 4$

11. What is the simplest form of $(5a - 3) - (6a - 4)$?　　　　11._____

　　A. $-a - 1$　　　B. $30a^2 + 12$　　　　C. $-a - 7$　　　　D. $-a + 1$

12. Which of the following shows the terms of $-1 + 4x^3 - 2x + 5x^5$　　12._____
　　 arranged so that the powers of "x" are in descending order?

　　A. $5x^5 + 4x^3 - 2x - 1$　　　　　　C. $5x^5 - 2x + 4x^3 - 1$

　　B. $4x^3 - 2x + 5x^5 - 1$　　　　　　D. $-1 - 2x + 4x^3 + 5x^5$

13. What is the simplest form of $-3(2n^2 - 6n) - 4(3n + 5)$?　　13._____

　　A. $-6n^2 + 6n - 20$　　　　　　C. $-6n^2 - 30n + 20$

　　B. $-6n^2 + 6n + 20$　　　　　　D. 20

14. What is the simplest form of $(x - 2)(x + 4)$?　　　　14._____

　　A. $x^2 + 2$　　　B. $x^2 - 8$　　　　C. $x^2 - 2x - 8$　　　D. $x^2 + 2x - 8$

15. What is the simplest form of $(3p - 4)(2p + 1)$?　　　　15._____

　　A. $6p^2 - 4$　　　　　　　　　C. $6p^2 - 5p - 3$

　　B. $6p^2 - 5p - 4$　　　　　　　D. $6p^2 - 11p - 4$

Polynomials Unit Review 1 *(cont.)*

16. What is the simplest form of $(2a - 3)(2a + 3)$? **16.**_____

    A. $4a^2$ **B.** $4a^2 - 9$ **C.** $6a^2 - 9$ **D.** $4a^2 - 6a$

17. What is the simplest form of $(x + 1)^2$? **17.**_____

    A. $x^2 + 2x + 1$ **B.** $x^2 + 2$ **C.** $x^2 + 1$ **D.** $x^2 + 2x + 2$

18. Find the solution of $4(2n - 3) = 6(2n + 2)$. **18.**_____

    A. $\dfrac{6}{5}$ **B.** $-\dfrac{6}{5}$ **C.** 6 **D.** -6

19. The length of a rectangle is 3 feet longer than the width. The area **19.**_____
of the rectangle is 54 square feet. If "w" is the width of the rectangle,
which equation is true?

    A. $w + w + 3 = 54$ **C.** $w(w + 3) = 54$
    B. $4w + 6 = 54$ **D.** $4w = 54$

20. The area of a square is $100\,\text{cm}^2$. If "x" is the length of one side, **20.**_____
which equation is true?

    A. $x + x = 100$ **C.** $4x = 100$
    B. $2x = 100$ **D.** $x^2 = 100$

Name _____

Polynomials Unit Review 2

Directions: Show your work neatly on another piece of paper.

1. What is the simplest form of $a^5 \cdot a^8$?   1._____

    A. a^{13} **B.** $2a^{13}$ **C.** a^3 **D.** $2a^3$

2. What is the simplest form of $(-4mn^2)(3mn^3)$?   2._____

    A. $12m^2n^5$ **B.** $-12m^2n^5$ **C.** $-m^2n^5$ **D.** $-12mn^5$

3. What is the simplest form of $(2xy^2)(3x^2y)^3$?   3._____

    A. $54x^7y^5$ **B.** $54x^6y^2$ **C.** $6x^7y^5$ **D.** $6x^6y^2$

4. What is the simplest form of $(3x^3)^2 + (4x^2)^3$?   4._____

    A. $9x^9 + 64x^8$ **B.** $73x^{12}$ **C.** $32x^5$ **D.** $73x^6$

5. What is the simplest form of $\dfrac{3p^4n^2}{9pn^3}$? (Assume that the denominator   5._____

  is not equal to zero.)

    A. $\dfrac{p^3}{6n}$ **B.** $\dfrac{p^5}{3n^5}$ **C.** $\dfrac{p^3}{3n}$ **D.** $\dfrac{p^5}{6n^5}$

6. What is the simplest form of $\dfrac{4m^{-2}n}{12mn^{-4}}$? (Assume that the denominator   6._____

  is not equal to zero.)

    A. $\dfrac{n^5}{8m^3}$ **B.** $\dfrac{m}{3n^3}$ **C.** $\dfrac{n^5}{3m^3}$ **D.** $\dfrac{m^3n^5}{3}$

7. What is 3.5×10^{-8} expressed in standard notation?   7._____

    A. 350,000,000   **C.** .0000035

    B. .000000035   **D.** 35,000,000

Polynomials Unit Review 2 *(cont.)*

8. What is the value of $(2 \times 10^7)(1 \times 10^3)$?　　　　　　　**8.**_____

    A. 3×10^{10}　　　　**B.** 2×10^4　　　　**C.** 2×10^{11}　　　　**D.** 2×10^{10}

9. What is the simplest form of $-3(4p)^2(4p^2)$?　　　　　　　**9.**_____

    A. $4p^5$　　　　　　**B.** $-192p^2$　　　　　**C.** $-48p^5$　　　　　**D.** $-192p^4$

10. What is the simplest form of $(4p^2 - 3p + 2) + (6p^2 - 3p - 5)$?　　　　　**10.**_____

    A. $10p^2 - 6p - 3$　　　　　　**C.** $10p^2 - 3$

    B. $10p^4 - 3$　　　　　　　　**D.** $10p^4 - 6p^2 - 3$

11. What is the simplest form of $(6m^2 - 3m + 2) - (4m^2 - 6m + 2)$?　　　　**11.**_____

    A. $2m^2 - 9m + 4$　　**B.** $2m^4 + 3m^2$　　　**C.** $2m^2 - 3m - 2$　　**D.** $2m^2 + 3m$

12. Which of the following shows the terms of $4a^5 + 6 + 3a^3 - 4a$　　　**12.**_____
    arranged so that the powers of "a" are in descending order?

    A. $6 + 4a^5 - 4a + 3a^3$　　　　　**C.** $6 - 4a + 3a^3 + 4a^5$

    B. $4a^5 + 3a^3 - 4a + 6$　　　　　**D.** $-4a + 3a^3 + 4a^5 + 6$

13. What is the simplest form of $-5a(3a^2 - 6a) - 4(2a^2 - 4a)$?　　　**13.**_____

    A. $-15a^3 - 38a^2 + 16a$　　　　**C.** $-15a^3 - 22a^2 + 16a$

    B. $-15a^3 + 22a^2 + 16a$　　　　**D.** $-15a^3 + 22a^4 + 16a$

14. What is the simplest form of $(p - 5)(p - 6)$?　　　　　**14.**_____

    A. $p^2 + 30$　　　　　　　**C.** $p^2 - 11p + 30$

    B. $p^2 + 11p + 30$　　　　　**D.** $p^2 - 11p - 11$

15. What is the simplest form of $(6a - 2)(6a + 1)$?　　　　　**15.**_____

    A. $36a^2 - 6a - 1$　　　　　**C.** $36a^2 - 6a - 2$

    B. $36a^2 - 18a - 2$　　　　　**D.** $36a^2 - 2$

Polynomials Unit Review 2 *(cont.)*

16. What is the simplest form of $(3a - 1)(3a + 1)$?

16._____

    A. $9a^2$ **C.** $9a^2 - 6a - 1$

    B. $9a^2 - 1$ **D.** $6a^2 - 1$

17. What is the simplest form of $(2x + 1)^2$?

17._____

    A. $4x^2 + 2x + 1$ **C.** $4x^2 + 1$

    B. $4x^2 + 4x + 2$ **D.** $4x^2 + 4x + 1$

18. Find the solution of $6n(3n + 2) = 3n(6n + 5) - 3$.

18._____

    A. 1   **B.** -1 **C.** 0   **D.** 2

19. The width of a rectangle is 3 meters less than the length. The area of the rectangle is $550\,m^2$. If "x" is the length of the rectangle, which equation is true?

19._____

    A. $2(x) + 2(x - 3) = 550$ **C.** $(3 - x)x = 550$

    B. $x + x - 3 = 550$ **D.** $x(x - 3) = 550$

20. The area of a rectangle is 900 square feet. The length is five more than twice the width. If "w" represents the width of the rectangle, which equation is true?

20._____

    A. $w + 2w + 5 = 900$ **C.** $w(2w + 5) = 900$

    B. $2(w) + 2(2w + 5) = 900$ **D.** $2w + 5 = 900$

Name _____

Dimensions of Rectangles

Directions: Find the dimensions and area of each rectangle.

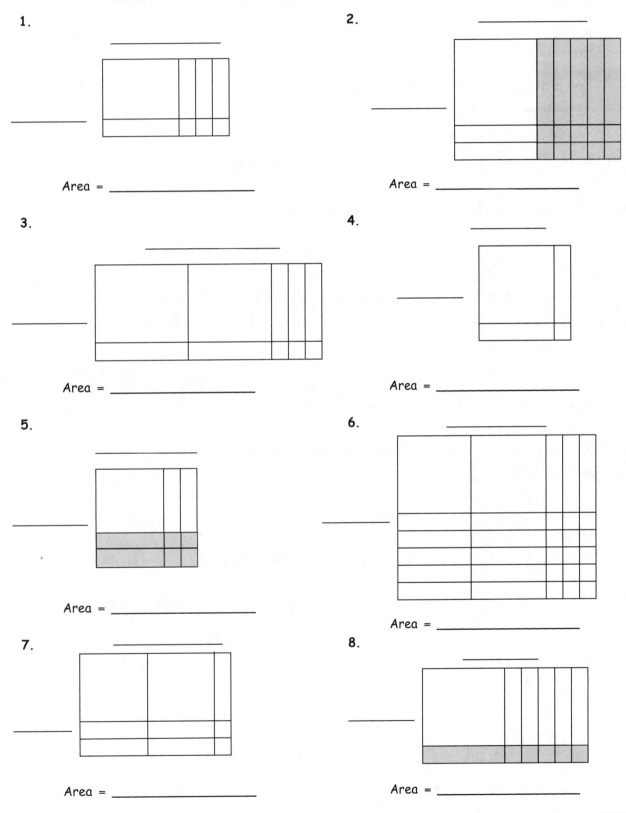

1.

Area = _____

2.

Area = _____

3.

Area = _____

4.

Area = _____

5.

Area = _____

6.

Area = _____

7.

Area = _____

8.

Area = _____

Teacher Created Materials
PUBLISHING

Dimensions of Rectangles *(cont.)*

Directions: Given the area, find the dimensions of each rectangle by factoring.

9.

$$a^2 + 2a - 15$$

_____

10.

$$m^2 - 49$$

_____

11.

$$6m^2 - 7m - 5$$

_____

12.

$$c^2 - 36$$

_____

13.

$$a^2 - 10ab + 21b$$

_____

14.

$$3e^2 - 2e - 21$$

_____

15.

$$2a^2 - 11a + 12$$

_____

16.

$$e^2 - 5e$$

_____

17.

$$w^2 - 5w$$

_____

Directions: Use the following picture to answer questions 18–21.

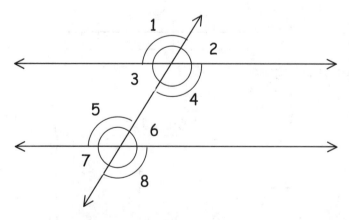

18. List all vertical angles.

19. List all corresponding angles.

20. List all alternate interior angles.

21. List all alternate exterior angles.

Name _____

Geometry Review (Factoring Unit)

Directions: Find the length of each missing side.

1. $P = 18m^2 - 3m + 2$

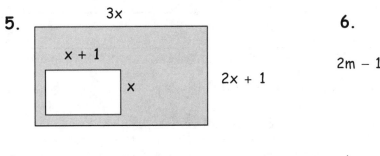

2. $P = 8x + 10$

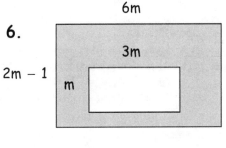

Directions: Find the measure of each missing angle.

3.

4.

Directions: Find the area of each shaded region.

5.

6.

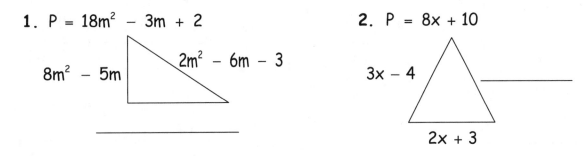

A = _____

A = _____

Directions: Find the area and perimeter of each figure.

7.

8.

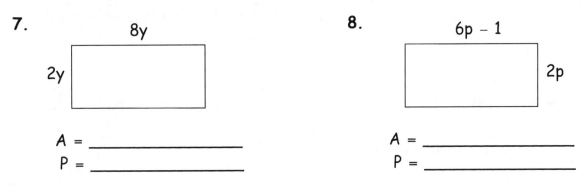

A = _____

P = _____

A = _____

P = _____

Geometry Review (Factoring Unit) *(cont.)*

Directions: Given the area, find the dimensions of each rectangle by factoring.

9.

$x^2 - 4x$

_____

10.

$3a^2 - a - 2$

_____

Directions: Find the dimensions and area of each rectangle.

11.

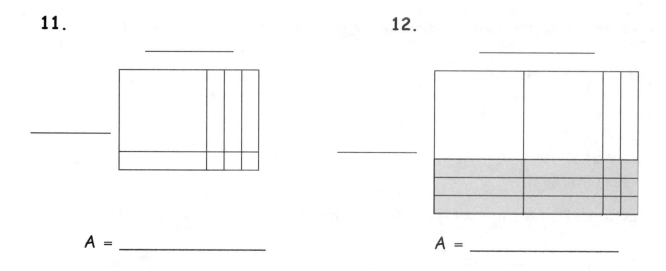

A = _____

12.

A = _____

Directions: List all pairs of vertical angles, corresponding angles, alternate interior angles, and alternate exterior angles.

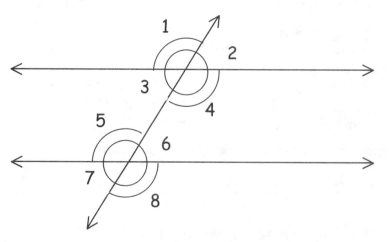

13. Vertical angles

14. Corresponding angles

15. Alternate interior angles

16. Alternate exterior angles

Teacher Created Materials
PUBLISHING

#10623—Active Algebra—Algebra I, Guided Practice Book

Name _____

Factoring Unit Review 1

Directions: Solve the following factoring problems.

1. Find the GCF of 3mn, 5xy, and 7ny.　　　　　　　　　1._____

2. What is the prime factorization of 180?　　　　　　　2._____

3. Find the GCF of $17m^2n$ and $15mn^2$.　　　　　　　3._____

4. Factor $6x + 2$.　　　　　　　　　　　　　　　　4._____

   A. $2(x + 1)$　　**B.** $2(3x + 1)$　　**C.** $6(x + 3)$　　**D.** $2(3x)$

5. Factor $4x^2 - 1$.　　　　　　　　　　　　　　　5._____

   A. $(2x + 1)(2x + 1)$　　　　**C.** $(2x + 1)(2x - 1)$
   B. $(4x - 1)(x + 1)$　　　　　**D.** $4(x^2 - 1)$

6. Factor $n^2 + n$.　　　　　　　　　　　　　　　6._____

   A. $n(n + n)$　　**B.** $n(n)$　　　**C.** $n(n + 1)$　　**D.** $2n(n + 1)$

7. Factor $6x^2 - 7x - 20$.　　　　　　　　　　　　7._____

   A. $(3x - 4)(2x + 5)$　　　　**C.** $(3x + 2)(2x - 10)$
   B. $(2x - 5)(3x + 4)$　　　　**D.** $(3x - 4)(2x - 5)$

8. Factor completely. $12x^2 - 2x - 2$　　　　　　　　8._____

   A. $(6x + 2)(2x - 1)$　　　　**C.** $2(3x + 1)(2x - 1)$
   B. $(4x - 2)(3x + 1)$　　　　**D.** $(6x + 1)(2x - 2)$

9. If $4p^2 - 8p - 5$ is factored, one of the factors is　　9._____

   A. $4p + 5$.　　**B.** $2p - 1$.　　**C.** $4p - 1$.　　**D.** $2p - 5$.

10. If $18x^2 + 15x + 2$ is factored, one of the factors is　　10._____

   A. $6x + 1$.　　**B.** $6x + 2$.　　**C.** $2x + 2$.　　**D.** $3x + 1$.

Factoring Unit Review 1 (cont.)

11. Which polynomial is prime?   11._____

    A. $x^2 - 1$ **B.** $4m^2 - 49$ **C.** $2n + 8$ **D.** $c^2 + 1$

12. Factor $y^4 - 1$ completely.   12._____

    A. $(y^2 + 1)(y - 1)(y + 1)$ **C.** $(y^4 - 1)(y + 1)$
    B. $(y^2 + 1)(y^2 - 1)$ **D.** $(y^2 - 1)(y^2 - 1)$

13. If $18x^2 - 18x - 8$ is factored completely, one of the factors is   13._____

    A. $6x + 2.$ **B.** $6x - 8.$ **C.** $3x - 4.$ **D.** $9x - 4.$

14. Each of the following is a perfect square trinomial except   14._____

    A. $4x^2 + 4x + 1.$ **C.** $4x^2 + 4x - 1.$
    B. $4x^2 - 12x + 9.$ **D.** $x^2 + 2x + 1.$

15. What is the solution set of the equation $(3a - 1)(2a + 5) = 0$?   15._____

    A. $\{\frac{1}{3}, -\frac{5}{2}\}$ **B.** $\{-\frac{1}{3}, \frac{5}{2}\}$ **C.** $\{3, \frac{2}{5}\}$ **D.** $\{-3, \frac{2}{5}\}$

16. What is the solution set of the equation $(4p - 3)(p + 1) = 0$?   16._____

    A. $\{\frac{3}{4}, 1\}$ **B.** $\{-\frac{3}{4}, -1\}$ **C.** $\{\frac{3}{4}, -1\}$ **D.** $\{\frac{4}{3}, -1\}$

17. What is the solution set of the equation $8x^2 - 2x = 3$?   17._____

    A. $\{-2, -\frac{4}{3}\}$ **B.** $\{\frac{1}{2}, -\frac{3}{4}\}$ **C.** $\{\frac{4}{3}, 2\}$ **D.** $\{\frac{3}{4}, -\frac{1}{2}\}$

18. What is the solution set of the equation $m^2 - 9m = 0$?   18._____

    A. $\{0, 9\}$ **B.** $\{1, 9\}$ **C.** $\{0, -9\}$ **D.** $\{9, -9\}$

19. The width of a rectangle is 4 cm less than the length. The area of the   19._____
rectangle is 525 cm². What is the width?

    A. 25 cm   **B.** 21 cm   **C.** 15 cm   **D.** 20 cm

20. The area of a square is 400 ft². Which of the following equations is   20._____
true?

    A. $2(x) = 400$ **B.** $4x = 400$ **C.** $x + x = 400$ **D.** $x^2 = 400$

Name _____

Factoring Unit Review 2

Directions: Solve the following factoring problems.

1. Find the GCF of $6xy$, $5xz$, and $7xw$.

   1._____

2. What is the prime factorization of 360?

   2._____

3. Find the GCF of $36a^3b^4$ and $12ab^2$.

   3._____

4. Factor completely. $3x^2 - 6x$

   4._____

   A. $3(x^2 - 2x)$
   C. $6x(x^2 - 3)$
   B. $3x^2(x - 2)$
   D. $3x(x - 2)$

5. Factor $9x^2 - 25$.

   5._____

   A. $(3x + 5)(3x - 5)$
   C. $(3x - 5)(3x - 5)$
   B. $(9x + 5)(x - 5)$
   D. $(3x + 5)(3x + 5)$

6. Factor completely. $6p^2 - 30p$

   6._____

   A. $6p(p - 5)$
   C. $6p(p - 5p)$
   B. $2(3p^2 - 15p)$
   D. $3p(2p - 10)$

7. Factor. $10x^2 - 17x + 3$

   7._____

   A. $(5x - 4)(2x - 3)$
   C. $(5x + 1)(2x + 3)$
   B. $(5x - 1)(2x + 3)$
   D. $(5x - 1)(2x - 3)$

8. Factor completely. $6p^3 - 25p^2 + 14p$

   8._____

   A. $p(6p - 7)(1p - 2)$
   C. $p(2p - 7)(3p - 2)$
   B. $p(2p + 7)(1p - 2)$
   D. $p(2p - 7)(3p + 2)$

9. If $4x^2 + 7x + 3$ is factored, one of the factors is

   9._____

   A. $2x + 4$.
   C. $4x + 2$.
   B. $3x + 4$.
   D. $4x + 3$.

10. If $6x^2 - x - 15$ is factored, one of the factors is

    10._____

    A. $6x + 1$.
    C. $3x + 5$.
    B. $3x - 3$.
    D. $2x + 3$

Factoring Unit Review 2 (cont.)

11. Which polynomial is prime?

    A. $4x^2 - 1$

    B. $3x^2 - 2x + 1$

    C. $4x^2 + 4x + 1$

    D. $2x^2 + 6x$

11._____

12. Factor completely. $16x^4 - 1$

    A. $(4x^2 + 1)(4x^2 - 1)$

    B. $(4x^2 - 1)(2x + 1)(2x - 1)$

    C. $(2x + 1)^2 (2x - 1)^2$

    D. $(4x^2 + 1)(2x + 1)(2x - 1)$

12._____

13. Factor completely. $16x^2 + 20x - 6$

    A. $2(4x - 1)(2x + 3)$

    B. $2(2x + 1)(2x + 3)$

    C. $(8x - 2)(2x + 3)$

    D. $(4x - 1)(4x + 6)$

13._____

14. Each of the following is a perfect square trinomial except

    A. $4x^2 + 12x + 9.$

    B. $9x^2 + 6x - 1.$

    C. $x^2 + 10x + 25.$

    D. $4x^2 - 4x + 1.$

14._____

15. What is the solution set of the equation $(3a - 1)(2a + 5) = 0$?

    A. $\{-\frac{1}{3}, \frac{5}{2}\}$

    B. $\{3, -\frac{5}{2}\}$

    C. $\{\frac{1}{3}, -\frac{5}{2}\}$

    D. $\{1, 5\}$

15._____

16. What is the solution set of the equation $(x - 5)(3x - 5) = 0$?

    A. $\{\frac{3}{5}, 5\}$

    B. $\{-5, -\frac{5}{3}\}$

    C. $\{-\frac{5}{3}, 5\}$

    D. $\{5, \frac{5}{3}\}$

16._____

17. What is the solution set of the equation $8p^2 + 2p = 3$?

    A. $\{\frac{3}{4}, \frac{1}{2}\}$

    B. $\{\frac{4}{3}, 2\}$

    C. $\{-\frac{3}{4}, \frac{1}{2}\}$

    D. $\{4, -2\}$

17._____

18. What is the solution set of the equation $m^2 - 6m = 0$?

    A. $\{0, 6\}$

    B. $\{0, -6\}$

    C. $\{6, -6\}$

    D. $\{0, \frac{1}{6}\}$

18._____

19. The area of a square is 169 cm^2. If "x" represents a side, which of the following equations is true?

    A. $4x = 169$

    B. $x^2 - 169 = 0$

    C. $2x = 169$

    D. $x + x = 169$

19._____

20. The length of a rectangle is 14 more than the width. The area of the rectangle is 275 m^2. What is the length?

    A. 11 m

    B. 24 m

    C. 25 m

    D. 31 m

20._____

Name _____

Applications 1

Directions: Solve. Show your work.

1. The length of a rectangle is 7 cm more than the width.
   The area of the rectangle is 120 cm².   Show work here.

    A. Assign variables.

       Let _____ = _____

          _____ = _____

    B. Draw the picture.

    C. Write an equation. _____

    D. Solve the equation to find length and width. _____

    E. Find the area of the rectangle numerically. _____

    F. Find the perimeter numerically. _____

    G. Find the perimeter algebraically. _____

2. The side of an equilateral triangle is $(4a - 1)$ inches.   Show work here.

    A. Draw the picture.

    B. Write an equation if the perimeter is 33 inches. _____

    C. Solve for "a." a = _____

    D. Find the length of one side numerically. _____

Applications 1 *(cont.)*

3. The length of a side of a square picture frame is (2x + 1) cm.
    The length of the square picture inside the frame is x cm.

    Show work here.

    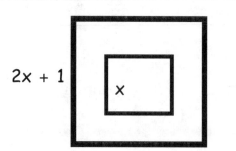

    2x + 1

    x

    A. Color the frame.

    B. Write an expression that describes the area of the picture frame.

    _____

    C. Simplify. _____

    _____

    D. If x = 4, find the area of the large square numerically. _____

    E. If x = 4, find the perimeter of the large square numerically. _____

    F. Find the perimeter of the large square algebraically. _____

4. Sally spends (x + 4) on gasoline each month. If her monthly salary is
    (10x + 2), how much is left after she pays the gasoline bill?

    A. Set up the problem. _____

    B. How much does she have left after she pays for gasoline (algebraically)?

    _____

    C. If she earns $806 a month, find "x." _____

    D. How much does she spend on gasoline? _____

    E. How much money does she have left? _____

Name _____

Applications 2

Directions: Solve. Show your work.

1. The length of a side of a square is $(3p - 1)$ cm.

   A. Draw the square.

   B. Write the equations for area and perimeter.
      A = _____
      P = _____

   C. If p = 5, what is the value of one side? _____

   D. If p = 5, find the area numerically. _____

   E. Find the perimeter numerically. _____

2. A rectangle has a length of $(m + 1)$ inches and a width of $(m - 2)$ inches.

   A. Draw the picture.   Show work here.

   B. Write an equation if the perimeter is 22 inches. _____

   C. Solve for "m." m = _____

   D. Find the length and the width numerically. _____

   E. Represent the area algebraically. _____

   F. What is the area numerically? _____

Applications 2 (cont.)

3. Write an expression that describes the area of the entire rectangle with the given dimensions.

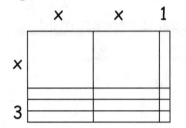

    A. What are the dimensions algebraically? _____ _____

    B. What is the area algebraically? _____

    C. What is the perimeter algebraically? _____

4. The perimeter of a square is (8x − 8) feet.

    Show work here.

    A. Draw the picture.

    B. Write an equation if the area is 16 square feet. _____

    C. Solve for x. _____

    D. What is the length numerically? _____

    E. Find the perimeter algebraically. _____

    F. Find the area numerically. _____

Name _____

Applications 3

Directions: Solve. Show your work.

1. Bart found that 1 side of his square swimming pool is represented by $(x + 2)$ feet.

A. Draw a picture.

B. Write an expression for the area. _____

C. Write an equation if the area is 64 square feet. _____

D. Solve for "x." x = _____

E. What is the numerical area? _____

F. What is the numerical perimeter? _____

G. What is the algebraic perimeter? _____

H. Write an equation for the perimeter. _____

2. The length of a rectangle is 5 meters more than three times the width. The area is 232 m^2.

Show work here.

A. Assign the variable.

   Let _____ = _____

   _____ = _____

B. Draw the picture.

C. Write an equation. _____

D. Solve for the length and width numerically. _____   _____

E. Find the area of the rectangle numerically. _____

F. Find the perimeter of the rectangle numerically. _____

Teacher Created Materials
PUBLISHING

Applications 3 *(cont.)*

3. The hypotenuse of a right triangle is 25 meters. One leg is 17 meters more than the other leg.

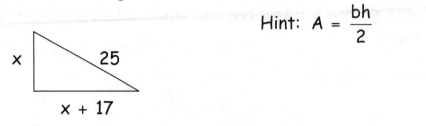

Hint: $A = \dfrac{bh}{2}$

A. Write an algebraic expression for the area. _____

B. If $x = 7$, find the perimeter numerically. _____

C. If $x = 7$, find the area numerically. _____

D. Write an algebraic expression for the perimeter. _____

4. The area of a square is $(4x^2 + 12x + 9)$ square feet.

A. Draw the picture.

B. Find the length and width algebraically. _____   _____

C. Find the algebraic expression that represents the perimeter.

_____

Teacher Created Materials
PUBLISHING

#10623—*Active Algebra—Algebra I, Guided Practice Book*

Name _____

Applications 4

Directions: Solve. Show your work.

1. The perimeter of the quadrilateral below is represented by (8x + 6y) meters.

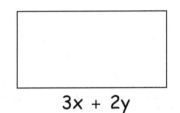

    3x + 2y

    A. What is the length of the missing side? _____

    B. Find the area algebraically. _____

    C. If x = 4 and y = 6, find the perimeter numerically. _____

    D. If x = 4 and y = 6, find the area numerically. _____

2. Ashley wants to enclose a small garden next to her house. She plans to use a total of 48 meters of fencing and the house as one of the sides. The variable "x" represents the length of the sides perpendicular to the house.

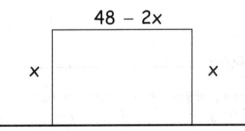

    48 – 2x

    x   x

    Write an equation for the area. A = _____

Applications 4 *(cont.)*

3. The height of a triangle is 7 meters less than the base. The area is 60 square meters. (Hint: $A = \dfrac{bh}{2}$)

   A. Let ___b___ = _____

      _____ = _____

   B. Draw the picture.

   C. Write an equation. _____

   D. Solve for "b." b = _____

   E. Use those numbers to show the area is 60 square meters.

      (Hint: $A = \dfrac{bh}{2}$) _____

4. The perimeter of the regular trapezoid below is (26x + 6) feet. The bases of the trapezoid are shown below. [Hint: $A = \dfrac{1}{2}(b_1 + b_2)h$]

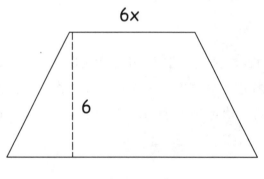

   6x

   6

   12x + 2

   A. Write an expression used to find the length of each side.

      _____

   B. What is the length of each missing side algebraically?

      _____

   C. If x = 4, find the area numerically. A =

      _____

Teacher Created Materials
PUBLISHING

Name _____

Applications 5

Directions: Solve. Show your work.

1. One rectangle is $(4x + 3)$ inches long and $(x + 2)$ inches wide. A second rectangle is $(2x + 1)$ inches long and $(x - 1)$ inches wide.

   A. Draw and label the picture.

   B. Write an expression that represents the difference of their areas.

   _____

   C. What is the difference in area?_____

   D. If $x = 5$, what are the dimensions of the 1st rectangle? _____

   E. If $x = 5$, what are the dimensions of the 2nd? _____

   F. Algebraic area of 1st _____   Numeric area of 1st _____

   G. Algebraic area of 2nd _____   Numeric area of 2nd _____

   H. Algebraic perimeter of 1st _____
       Numeric perimeter of 1st _____

   I. Algebraic perimeter of 2nd _____
       Numeric perimeter of 2nd _____

2. Express the sum of the areas of the rectangles below as a polynomial.

   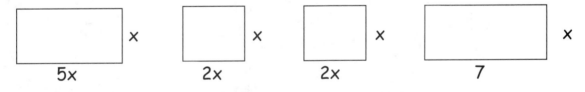

   | 5x | 2x | 2x | 7 |

   A. What is the sum of the areas?_____

   B. What is the sum of the perimeters?_____

   C. What is the area of the 1st two rectangles minus the area of the 2nd two rectangles? _____

   D. If $x = 3$, find the sum of the perimeters. _____

   E. If $x = 3$, find the total area of all rectangles. _____

Teacher Created Materials
PUBLISHING

Applications 5 *(cont.)*

3. The perimeter of the rectangle below is 50 inches and can be represented

    by the formula $P = 2\left(\dfrac{60}{x}\right) + 2\left(\dfrac{90}{x}\right)$.

    Show work here.

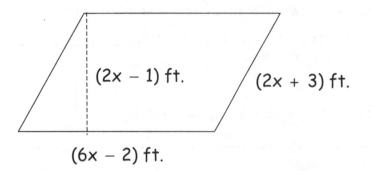

$\dfrac{60}{x}$

$\dfrac{90}{x}$

  A. Write an equation. _____

  B. Find "x." x = _____

  C. Use x to find the perimeter numerically. _____

  D. Use x to find the area numerically. _____

4. Find the perimeter of the parallelogram below. (Hint: A = bh)

$(2x - 1)$ ft.

$(2x + 3)$ ft.

$(6x - 2)$ ft.

  A. Find the perimeter algebraically. _____

  B. Find the area algebraically. _____

  C. If x = 4, find the perimeter numerically. _____

  D. If x = 4, find the area numerically. _____

Name _____

Applications 6

Directions: Solve. Show your work.

1. The length of a side of a square picture frame is (3x + 1) cm. The length of the square picture inside the frame is x cm.

3x + 1

Show work here.

    A. Color the frame.

    B. Write an expression that describes the area of the picture frame.

    _____

    _____

    C. Simplify. _____

    D. If x = 4, find the area of the large square. _____

    E. If x = 4, find the numeric perimeter of the large square. _____

    F. Find the algebraic perimeter of the large square. _____

2. The product of x + 5 and x + 8 is 180 square yards.

    A. Write an equation. _____

    B. Solve for "x." x = _____

    C. What does 180 square yards represent in relation to a rectangle?

    _____

Applications 6 *(cont.)*

3. A 6-foot by 3-foot table is placed on a square lawn whose side is x feet long.

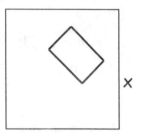

x

A. Label the picture.

B. Write an expression that represents the area of the lawn not covered by the table. _____

C. If x = 10, find the area of the lawn not covered by the table. _____

D. If x = 10, find the numeric perimeter of the large square. _____

E. Find the numeric area of the small rectangle. _____

4. The area of a rectangular swimming pool is 266 m^2. The length of the swimming pool is 5 meters more than its width.

Show work here.

A. Let _____ = _____

_____ = _____

B. Draw and label the picture.

C. Write an equation. _____

D. Solve for "w." w = _____

E. What is the numerical length? _____

F. What is the algebraic perimeter? _____

G. What is the area numerically? _____

Name _____

Simplifying Radicals 1

Directions: Simplify the following. Assume that all variables are nonnegative.

1. $\sqrt{32} =$ _____

2. $\sqrt{12} =$ _____

3. $\sqrt{20} =$ _____

4. $\sqrt{8} =$ _____

5. $\sqrt{25} =$ _____

6. $\sqrt{50} =$ _____

7. $\sqrt{48} =$ _____

8. $\sqrt{9} =$ _____

9. $\sqrt{10} =$ _____

10. $\sqrt{x^2} =$ _____

11. $\sqrt{x^4} =$ _____

12. $\sqrt{9p^4} =$ _____

13. $\sqrt{20x^2} =$ _____

14. $\sqrt{32x^6} =$ _____

15. $\sqrt{m^4 n^6} =$ _____

16. $\sqrt{50x^4 y^{10}} =$ _____

17. $\sqrt{13x^2} =$ _____

18. $\sqrt{75} =$ _____

19. $\sqrt{45} =$ _____

20. $\sqrt{300} =$ _____

21. $\sqrt{49} =$ _____

22. $\sqrt{125} =$ _____

23. $\sqrt{28} =$ _____

24. $\sqrt{200} =$ _____

25. $\sqrt{4} =$ _____

26. $\sqrt{100} =$ _____

27. $\sqrt{80} =$ _____

28. $\sqrt{12m^4} =$ _____

29. $\sqrt{100x^4} =$ _____

30. $\sqrt{45m^8} =$ _____

31. $\sqrt{49x^{10} y^{12}} =$ _____

32. $\sqrt{28p^2 q^6} =$ _____

33. $\sqrt{25m^6 n^{12}} =$ _____

34. $\sqrt{19p^{10}} =$ _____

Name _____

Simplifying Radicals 2

Directions: Simplify the following. Assume that all variables are nonnegative.

1. $\sqrt{98}$ = _____

2. $\sqrt{80}$ = _____

3. $-\sqrt{12}$ = _____

4. $3\sqrt{8}$ = _____

5. $\sqrt{121}$ = _____

6. $\sqrt{40}$ = _____

7. $4\sqrt{64}$ = _____

8. $\sqrt{10}$ = _____

9. $\sqrt{196}$ = _____

10. $\sqrt{x^4}$ = _____

11. $3\sqrt{x^7}$ = _____

12. $\sqrt{16p^6}$ = _____

13. $\sqrt{-75x}$ = _____

14. $\sqrt{32x^8}$ = _____

15. $4\sqrt{m^3n^9}$ = _____

16. $\sqrt{144x^4y^9}$ = _____

17. $-5\sqrt{13x^3}$ = _____

18. $\sqrt{500}$ = _____

19. $2\sqrt{54}$ = _____

20. $\sqrt{225}$ = _____

21. $\sqrt{150}$ = _____

22. $\sqrt{-150}$ = _____

23. $\sqrt{6}$ = _____

24. $\sqrt{45}$ = _____

25. $\sqrt{9}$ = _____

26. $5\sqrt{81}$ = _____

27. $\sqrt{90}$ = _____

28. $\sqrt{8m^5}$ = _____

29. $-2\sqrt{49x^4}$ = _____

30. $\sqrt{45m^{11}}$ = _____

31. $\sqrt{36x^8y^{12}}$ = _____

32. $-\sqrt{28p^5q^3}$ = _____

33. $3\sqrt{25m^7n^{14}}$ = _____

34. $\sqrt{19p^9}$ = _____

Name _____

Applications 7

Directions: Solve. Show your work.

1. Tate wants to enclose a small area by the garage for his dog, Mackie.
    He plans to use only 16 feet of fencing. The variable "x" represents the
    length of the sides perpendicular to the garage.

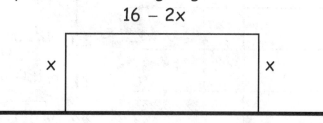

    A. Write an equation for area. A = _____

    B. How much fencing does Tate need (algebraically)? _____

    C. If x = 3, how much fencing does he need? _____

2. The length of the pool is 7 meters more than 4 times the width. The new
    tile sidewalk around the pool is 1 meter wide. What is the area covered by
    the pool and the sidewalk?

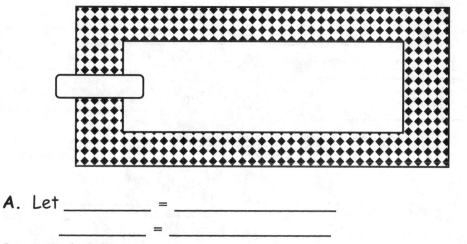

    A. Let _____ = _____

            _____ = _____

    B. Label the picture.

    C. What are the dimensions of the sidewalk?_____

    D. What is the area covered by the pool and the sidewalk? _____

Applications 7 (cont.)

3. A picture is x feet on each side. The outside of the frame is (x + 2) feet wide.

A. Label the picture.

B. Write an equation to describe the area of the picture only.
A = _____

C. Write an equation to describe the area of the framed picture.
A = _____

D. Write an expression to represent the shaded region.
_____

E. If the area of the framed picture is 36 square feet, write an equation. _____

F. Solve for "x." x = _____

Show work here.

G. What is the numeric perimeter of the large square? _____

H. What is the algebraic perimeter of the large square? _____

I. What is the numeric area of the large square? _____

J. What is the algebraic area of the small square? _____

Name _____

Area and Perimeter with Radicals

Directions: Find each perimeter.

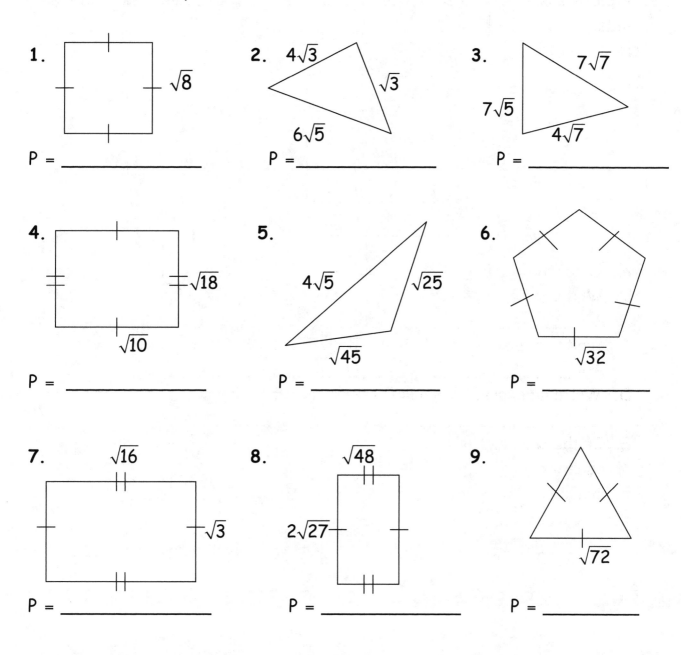

1.

P = _____

2. $4\sqrt{3}$ $\sqrt{3}$ $6\sqrt{5}$

P = _____

3. $7\sqrt{7}$ $7\sqrt{5}$ $4\sqrt{7}$

P = _____

4. $\sqrt{18}$ $\sqrt{10}$

P = _____

5. $4\sqrt{5}$ $\sqrt{25}$ $\sqrt{45}$

P = _____

6. $\sqrt{32}$

P = _____

7. $\sqrt{16}$ $\sqrt{3}$

P = _____

8. $\sqrt{48}$ $2\sqrt{27}$

P = _____

9. $\sqrt{72}$

P = _____

10. Draw a triangle with these sides and find the perimeter.

$\sqrt{8}$ cm

$2\sqrt{50}$ cm

$\sqrt{18}$ cm

P = _____

Teacher Created Materials PUBLISHING

Area and Perimeter with Radicals (cont.)

Directions: Find the area.

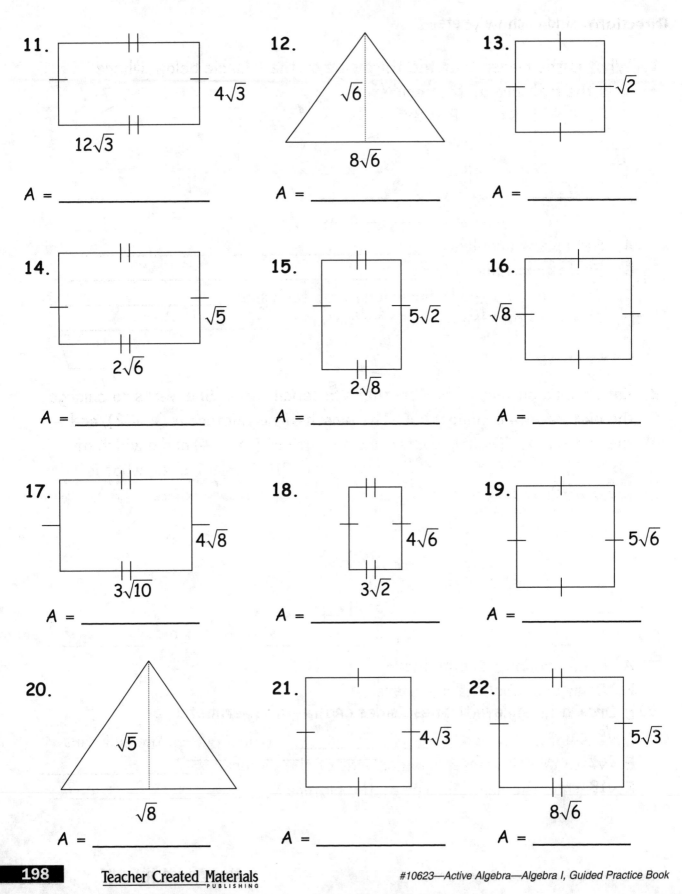

11. $4\sqrt{3}$ $12\sqrt{3}$

A = _____

12. $\sqrt{6}$ $8\sqrt{6}$

A = _____

13. $\sqrt{2}$

A = _____

14. $\sqrt{5}$ $2\sqrt{6}$

A = _____

15. $5\sqrt{2}$ $2\sqrt{8}$

A = _____

16. $\sqrt{8}$

A = _____

17. $4\sqrt{8}$ $3\sqrt{10}$

A = _____

18. $4\sqrt{6}$ $3\sqrt{2}$

A = _____

19. $5\sqrt{6}$

A = _____

20. $\sqrt{5}$ $\sqrt{8}$

A = _____

21. $4\sqrt{3}$

A = _____

22. $5\sqrt{3}$ $8\sqrt{6}$

A = _____

Name _____

Applications 8

Directions: Solve. Show your work.

1. What is the measure of the third side of the triangle below, where P is the measure of the perimeter?

$$P = 8x^2 - 3x$$

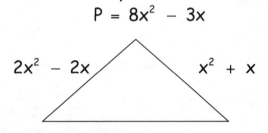

$2x^2 - 2x$ $\qquad$ $x^2 + x$

  A. Set up the problem. _____

  B. Find the missing side. _____

  C. If $x = 6$, find the numeric length of each side. _____

  D. If $x = 6$, find the numeric perimeter. _____

2. Kara took a picture of her brother's baseball team. She wants to enlarge the picture into a miniposter. The length of her picture is $(x + 2)$, and the width is x. The miniposter has a length of $(4x - 4)$ and a width of $(3x + 6)$. If the area of the miniposter is 216 square inches, what is the area of the picture?   Show work here.

  A. Draw and label the picture.

  B. Draw and label the miniposter.

  C. Write an equation for the area of the miniposter. _____

  D. Solve for "x." $x =$ _____ (Hint: Factor the GCF first.)

  E. What are the numeric dimensions of the picture?_____

  F. What is the numeric area of the picture? _____

Applications 8 (cont.)

3. The sum of the degree measures of the angles of a quadrilateral is 360°. What is the measure of the fourth angle if the other three angles measure $6x + 2$, $4x - 1$, and $x + 7$? (Hint: A quadrilateral has 4 sides.)

   A. Draw and label the picture.

   B. Set up the problem. _____

   _____

   C. Find the measure of the fourth angle (algebraically). _____
   D. If $x = 10$, find all angle measures. _____
   E. Find the numeric sum of all angle measures. _____

4. Takisha has a picture with a length 4 inches greater than its width. A frame 2 inches wide will be placed around the picture. The area of the picture and frame together is 525 square inches. How can the area of the picture and the frame best be represented?   Show work here.
   A. Let _____ = _____

   _____ = _____
   B. Draw and label the diagram.

   C. What are the dimensions of the frame? _____
   D. What is the algebraic area of the picture and frame together?

   _____
   E. Write an equation for the situation. _____
   F. Solve for "x." x = _____
   G. What is the numeric perimeter of the picture?_____
   H. What is the numeric area of the picture? _____
   I. What is the numeric perimeter of the frame? _____

Name _____

Geometry Review (Radicals and Quadratics Unit)

Directions: Solve.

1. Find the length of the missing side.

$P = 7x - 5$

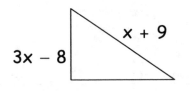

$x + 9$

$3x - 8$

_____

2. Find the value of the missing angle.

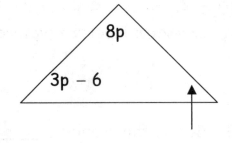

$8p$

$3p - 6$

_____

3. Find the area of the shaded region.

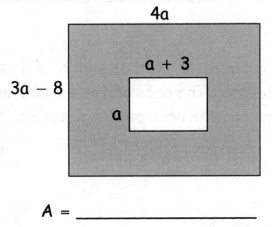

$4a$

$a + 3$

$3a - 8$

a

$A =$ _____

4. Find the area and the perimeter.

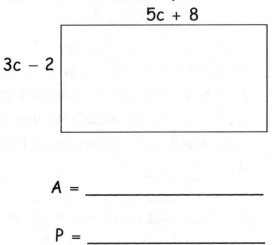

$5c + 8$

$3c - 2$

$A =$ _____

$P =$ _____

5. Given the area, find the dimensions of the rectangle.

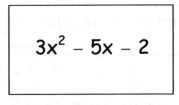

$3x^2 - 5x - 2$

_____

6. Find the dimensions and area of the rectangle.

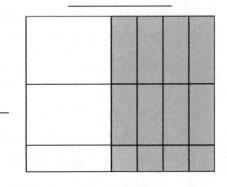

$A =$ _____

Geometry Review (Radicals and Quadratics Unit) *(cont.)*

Directions: Solve for the given variable, and find the measure of each angle.

7.

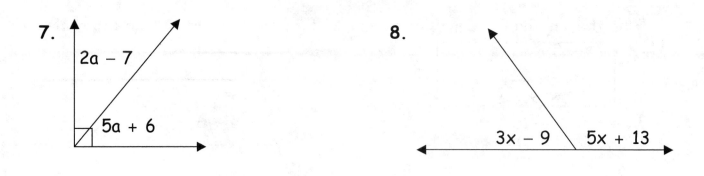

$2a - 7$

$5a + 6$

8.

$3x - 9$ $5x + 13$

9.

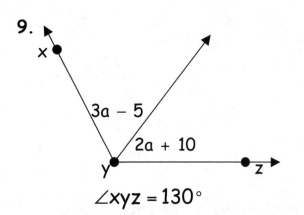

x

$3a - 5$

$2a + 10$

y   z

$\angle xyz = 130°$

10.

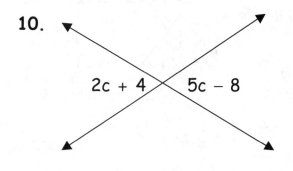

$2c + 4$ $5c - 8$

Teacher Created Materials
PUBLISHING

Geometry Review (Radicals and Quadratics Unit) *(cont.)*

Directions: Find the area and/or perimeter for each figure.

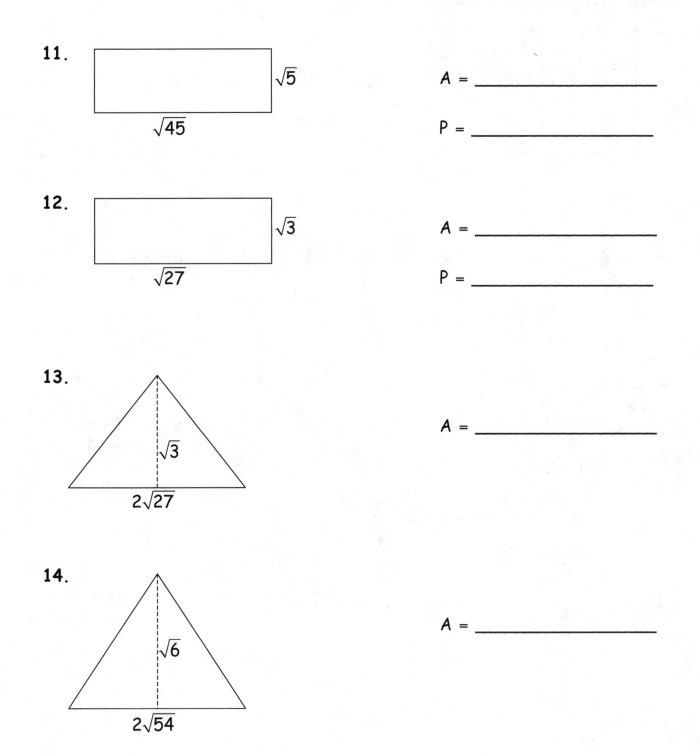

11.

$\sqrt{5}$

$\sqrt{45}$

A = _____

P = _____

12.

$\sqrt{3}$

$\sqrt{27}$

A = _____

P = _____

13.

$\sqrt{3}$

$2\sqrt{27}$

A = _____

14.

$\sqrt{6}$

$2\sqrt{54}$

A = _____

Name _____

Simplifying Quadratic Answers

Directions: Simplify the following.

1. $x = \dfrac{6 \pm 3\sqrt{7}}{9}$

2. $x = \dfrac{7 \pm \sqrt{49}}{7}$

3. $x = \dfrac{8 \pm 4\sqrt{2}}{6}$

4. $x = \dfrac{9 \pm \sqrt{72}}{12}$

5. $x = \dfrac{4 \pm \sqrt{32}}{8}$

6. $x = \dfrac{6 \pm \sqrt{50}}{6}$

7. $x = \dfrac{8 \pm \sqrt{147}}{2}$

8. $x = \dfrac{6 \pm \sqrt{8}}{2}$

9. $x = \dfrac{9 \pm \sqrt{27}}{3}$

10. $x = \dfrac{8 \pm \sqrt{20}}{4}$

11. $x = \dfrac{4 \pm \sqrt{16}}{2}$

12. $x = \dfrac{5 \pm \sqrt{36}}{4}$

Teacher Created Materials
PUBLISHING

#10623—*Active Algebra—Algebra I, Guided Practice Book*

Name _____

Quadratics Unit Review

Directions: Find the axis of symmetry, vertex, and graph of each function.

1. $y = 3x^2 - 6x + 1$ a = _____ b = _____ c = _____

Axis of Symmetry_____   Vertex (___,___) MAX or MIN?

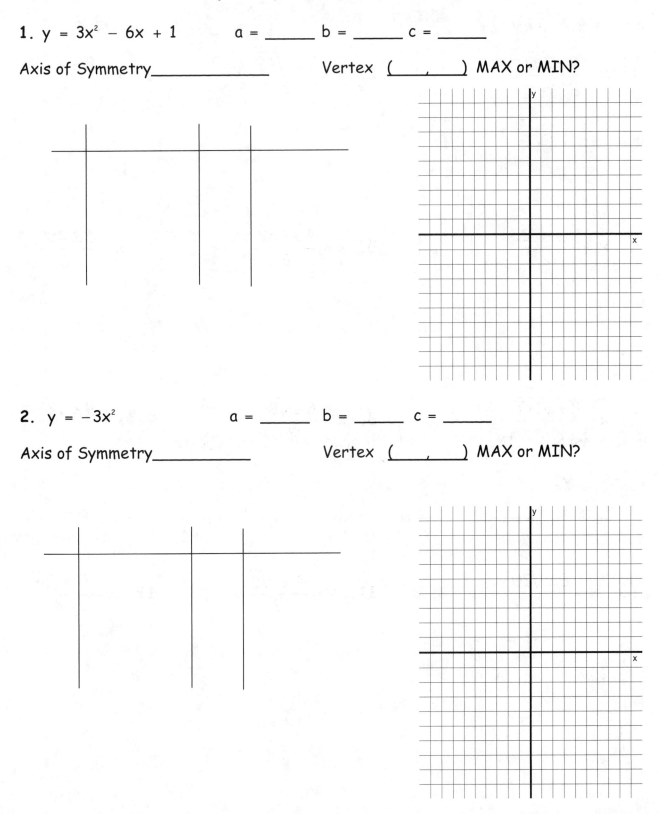

2. $y = -3x^2$ a = _____ b = _____ c = _____

Axis of Symmetry_____   Vertex (___,___) MAX or MIN?

Quadratics Unit Review (cont.)

3. $y = -2x^2 + 4x$ $a =$ _____ $b =$ _____ $c =$ _____

Axis of Symmetry _____   Vertex (___ , ___) MAX or MIN?

Directions: Solve. Use the quadratic formula or factor, whichever is valid.

4. $2x^2 + 7x - 4 = 0$

$a =$ _____ $b =$ _____ $c =$ _____

5. $x^2 + 6x + 7 = 0$

$a =$ _____ $b =$ _____ $c =$ _____

Teacher Created Materials
PUBLISHING

#10623—*Active Algebra—Algebra I, Guided Practice Book*

Quadratics Unit Review (cont.)

6. $2y^2 = 5y - 2$

a = _____ b = _____ c = _____

7. $2x^2 + 6x - 1 = 0$

a = _____ b = _____ c = _____

8. $3x^2 - 5x - 4 = 0$

a = _____ b = _____ c = _____

9. $y^2 - 2y = -1$

a = _____ b = _____ c = _____

10. $15n^2 - 5n = 0$

a = _____ b = _____ c = _____

Name _____

Simplifying Rational Expressions 1

Directions: Simplify. Assume that no denominator has a value of zero.

1. $\dfrac{x^2(x+2)}{6x^5}$ = _____

2. $\dfrac{(x+2)(x-3)}{x+2}$ = _____

3. $\dfrac{5m^2n(n-3)}{10m(n-3)}$ = _____

4. $\dfrac{2x^3y^3(x-2)}{6x^5y(2-x)}$ = _____

5. $\dfrac{2(x-3)}{2x+7}$ = _____

6. $\dfrac{3(x-2)}{6(x+2)}$ = _____

7. $\dfrac{x-1}{1-x}$ = _____

8. $\dfrac{3(m+6)}{2(m-4)}$ = _____

9. $\dfrac{4(m+8)}{6m}$ = _____

10. $\dfrac{3x(2x+5)}{6x^4(x+5)}$ = _____

11. $\dfrac{3(6x+5)}{3x+2}$ = _____

12. $\dfrac{4x(2x-1)}{5x(3x-1)}$ = _____

13. $\dfrac{2m^2n^5}{6m^5n}$ = _____

14. $\dfrac{8(k-3)}{6k}$ = _____

Teacher Created Materials
PUBLISHING

Name _____

Simplifying Rational Expressions 2

Directions: Simplify. Assume that no denominator has a value of zero.

1. $\dfrac{2x^2(x+4)}{6x^8} =$ _____

2. $\dfrac{(x+6)(x-5)}{x-5} =$ _____

3. $\dfrac{5v(2x+3)}{10v^2} =$ _____

4. $\dfrac{-6x^5y^2(x-2)}{3x^5y(x-2)} =$ _____

5. $\dfrac{h-2}{2-h} =$ _____

6. $\dfrac{2(x-9)}{4(x+9)} =$ _____

7. $\dfrac{(x+1)(x-1)}{x+1} =$ _____

8. $\dfrac{x+2}{x+2} =$ _____

9. $\dfrac{3(a+4)(4-a)}{9a(a-4)} =$ _____

10. $\dfrac{x(2x+3)}{2x^3(x+3)} =$ _____

11. $\dfrac{8(2x+5)}{3x+5} =$ _____

12. $\dfrac{4x(3x-1)}{6x(2x-1)} =$ _____

13. $\dfrac{4x^7y^3(x-2)}{12x^5y(2-x)} =$ _____

14. $\dfrac{7(a-6)}{21a} =$ _____

Name _____

Simplifying Rational Expressions 3

Directions: Simplify. Be sure to identify restrictions.

1. $\dfrac{x^2(x+4)(x+2)}{6x^8(x+2)(x-3)} = $ _____

8. $\dfrac{2(x-5)}{5-x} = $ _____

2. $\dfrac{(x+6)(x-5)(x-1)}{4(x-5)(1-x)} = $ _____

9. $\dfrac{3a^4(a+2)(a-4)}{12a-3a^2} = $ _____

3. $\dfrac{2z(2x+3)(3-x)}{10v^2z^2(x-3)} = $ _____

10. $\dfrac{8x^3(x-5)(x-6)}{2x^4(x-6)(5-x)} = $ _____

4. $\dfrac{2x^5y^2(x+2)}{-3x^5y(x-2)} = $ _____

11. $\dfrac{8(2x+5)}{6x+5} = $ _____

5. $\dfrac{6x^4(3x-1)(1-2x)}{6x(2x-1)} = $ _____

12. $\dfrac{x-3}{3-x} = $ _____

6. $\dfrac{2(x-2)(x-3)}{4(3-x)(x-2)} = $ _____

13. $\dfrac{x^2y^3(7-x)}{5x^3y(x+7)} = $ _____

7. $\dfrac{6(x+1)(x-1)(2-x)}{(x-2)(x+1)} = $ _____

14. $\dfrac{7c^6(c-2)}{21c^5(c+2)} = $ _____

Teacher Created Materials
PUBLISHING

Name _____

Simplifying Rational Expressions 4

Directions: Simplify. Be sure to identify restrictions.

1. $\dfrac{3x^5(x+4)}{9x^8(4-x)} =$ _____

2. $\dfrac{x^6(x+8)(x-2)}{2x^2-x^3} =$ _____

3. $\dfrac{15x^2(2x+3)(x-4)}{5x^3(3+2x)} =$ _____

4. $\dfrac{-5a^6b^2(3x-2)}{10a^5b^5(3x-2)} =$ _____

5. $\dfrac{6c-12}{(2-c)} =$ _____

6. $\dfrac{2(v-6)}{4(v+6)(v-6)} =$ _____

7. $\dfrac{(x-3)(x-1)}{(3-x)(x-2)} =$ _____

8. $\dfrac{(2-x)(x+3)}{(x+3)(x-2)} =$ _____

9. $\dfrac{7a^2(a-3)(a+4)}{10a(4+a)} =$ _____

10. $\dfrac{9x^3(x+2)(x-2)}{3x^2(x+2)} =$ _____

11. $\dfrac{x^2-25}{4(x+5)(5-x)} =$ _____

12. $\dfrac{5x^2(x-1)}{15x^2(2x-1)} =$ _____

13. $\dfrac{6x^3y^3(x-9)}{12x^5y^3(x+9)} =$ _____

14. $\dfrac{24x(x-4)}{8x^3} =$ _____

Teacher Created Materials
PUBLISHING

Name _____

Fractions Review

Directions: Calculate.

1. $\dfrac{4}{3}(5) - 8$

2. $\dfrac{2}{5} \div 3 - 6$

3. $-\dfrac{2}{3}(4) + 6$

4. $5 \div \left(-\dfrac{1}{2}\right) + 3$

5. $-\dfrac{3}{2}(6) - 4$

6. $7 \div \left(-\dfrac{3}{2}\right) + 2$

7. $-\dfrac{3}{4}\left(\dfrac{1}{2}\right) - \dfrac{1}{3}$

8. $-\dfrac{3}{7}(2) + \dfrac{2}{7}$

9. $-\dfrac{1}{6}\left(\dfrac{4}{5}\right) + 3$

10. $-\dfrac{1}{5}\left(\dfrac{4}{3}\right) - 6$

11. $-3 \div \left(-\dfrac{4}{7}\right) + 2$

12. $\dfrac{1}{8}\left(-\dfrac{3}{2}\right) - 3$

Teacher Created Materials PUBLISHING

Fractions Review *(cont.)*

13. $-6 \div \dfrac{1}{2} - 3$

14. $2\left(\dfrac{3}{2}\right) - 5$

15. $\dfrac{4}{5}\left(\dfrac{3}{8}\right) - \dfrac{5}{3}$

16. $-10 \div \dfrac{2}{3} - 7$

17. $-\dfrac{8}{9}\left(\dfrac{3}{4}\right) - 7$

18. $8 - \dfrac{1}{4}\left(\dfrac{2}{3}\right)$

19. $-6 - 3 \div \dfrac{1}{3}$

20. $-4\left(-\dfrac{1}{2}\right) + \dfrac{3}{4}$

Bonus: Solve.

$$\dfrac{\dfrac{3}{8}\left(\dfrac{2}{5}\right) - 3}{-\dfrac{1}{4}\left(\dfrac{7}{5}\right) - \dfrac{5}{2}}$$

Teacher Created Materials PUBLISHING

Name _____

Rational Expressions Mid-Unit Review

Directions: Calculate.

1. $\dfrac{5}{7} \div \left(\dfrac{-1}{2} \right) + 3$

2. $\dfrac{3}{7}(2) + \dfrac{2}{7}$

3. $7 \div \left(\dfrac{-3}{2} \right) + 2$

4. $\dfrac{8}{9}\left(\dfrac{3}{4} \right) - 7$

Directions: Simplify. Be sure to identify restrictions.

5. $\dfrac{6a^2b(a-4)}{9a^5b^3(a-4)}$

6. $\dfrac{2(x-2)}{4(2-x)}$

7. $\dfrac{p+1}{p-1}$

8. $\dfrac{a-b}{a^2-b^2}$

9. $\dfrac{2x+10}{x^2-25}$

10. $\dfrac{3m^2-27}{m^2+7m+12}$

Rational Expressions Mid-Unit Review (cont.)

11. $\dfrac{16x^3y}{3x^2} \cdot \dfrac{27y}{4x^2}$

12. $\dfrac{m-7}{m-2} \cdot \dfrac{m^2-4}{m-7}$

13. $\dfrac{a^2-16}{2a+8} \cdot \dfrac{a+4}{a^2+8a+16}$

14. $\dfrac{6m^2n}{8} \div 18mn$

15. $\dfrac{x^2-36}{x^2-49} \div \dfrac{x+6}{x-7}$

16. $\dfrac{3y^3-27y}{2y^2+5y-3} \div \dfrac{9y^2}{4y^2-1}$

17. $\dfrac{a^2-5a+6}{4} \div \dfrac{a-3}{16}$

Name _____

Adding and Subtracting Rational Expressions

Directions: Simplify. Assume that no denominator has a value of zero.

1. $\dfrac{4}{a} + \dfrac{10}{a}$

2. $\dfrac{p+5}{7} - \dfrac{p}{7}$

3. $\dfrac{c+4}{4} - \dfrac{c-4}{4}$

4. $\dfrac{8n}{2n+3} - \dfrac{-12}{2n+3}$

5. $\dfrac{3x}{3x+4} + \dfrac{4}{3x+4}$

6. $\dfrac{2}{p} + \dfrac{6}{2p}$

7. $\dfrac{1}{6a} + \dfrac{4}{8}$

8. $\dfrac{x}{x-3} - \dfrac{3}{x+3}$

9. $\dfrac{6}{c+1} + \dfrac{4}{c+2}$

10. $\dfrac{m}{5m+5} - \dfrac{1}{m+1}$

Teacher Created Materials
PUBLISHING

#10623—Active Algebra—Algebra I, Guided Practice Book

Name _____

Rational Expressions Unit Review 1

Directions: Show your work neatly on another sheet of paper.

1. Simplify $\dfrac{m^2 - 3m - 4}{m^2 - 5m + 4}$.

   A. 1   B. $\dfrac{m+1}{m-1}$ C. 0   D. $\dfrac{m-1}{m+1}$ 1._____

2. Simplify $\dfrac{6m^2 + 7m + 2}{6m^2 + 5m + 1}$.

   A. 1   B. $\dfrac{3m+2}{3m}$ C. $\dfrac{3m+2}{3m+1}$ D. $\dfrac{6m-1}{6m+1}$ 2._____

3. Find $\dfrac{8p^2y^3}{5m} \cdot \dfrac{10m^3}{6py}$.

   A. $\dfrac{8m^2py^2}{3}$ B. $\dfrac{2m^2py^2}{3}$ C. $\dfrac{4m^2py^2}{3}$ D. $\dfrac{8m^2y^2}{3}$ 3._____

4. What are the excluded values of "p" in $\dfrac{p+5}{p^2 - 36}$?

   A. $p \neq 1$ B. $p \neq -5$ C. $p \neq -6, -5, 6$ D. $p \neq -6, 6$ 4._____

5. What are the excluded values of "a" in $\dfrac{2a^2 + 9a + 4}{a^2 + 2a - 15}$?

   A. $a \neq 3, 5$ B. $a \neq -4, -\dfrac{1}{2}$ C. $a \neq -5, 3$ D. $a \neq -3, 5$ 5._____

6. Find $\dfrac{m^2 - 36}{6} \cdot \dfrac{8}{(m+6)^2}$.

   A. $\dfrac{4}{3}$ B. $-\dfrac{4}{3}$ C. $\dfrac{4(m-6)}{3}$ D. $\dfrac{4(m-6)}{3(m+6)}$ 6._____

7. Find $\dfrac{3x+6}{6x+3} \div \dfrac{4x+8}{4x^2 - 1}$.

   A. $\dfrac{2x-1}{4}$ B. $2x-1$ C. $\dfrac{3(2x-1)}{4}$ D. $\dfrac{2x+1}{4}$ 7._____

8. Find $\dfrac{6p^2}{12m^2n} \cdot \dfrac{8mn^3}{9p^5}$.

   A. $\dfrac{4n^2}{9mp^3}$ B. $\dfrac{n^2}{mp^3}$ C. $\dfrac{2n^2}{3mp^3}$ D. $\dfrac{4n^2}{mp^3}$ 8._____

Rational Expressions Unit Review 1 (cont.)

9. Find $\dfrac{2x-6}{x^2-9} \div \dfrac{4x-8}{3x+9}$.

A. $\dfrac{3}{2(x-2)}$ B. $\dfrac{1}{2(x-2)}$ C. $\dfrac{3}{x-2}$ D. $\dfrac{3}{2}$ 9._____

10. Find $\dfrac{m^2+m}{6m^2-6n^2} \cdot \dfrac{m+n}{m^3+m^2}$.

A. $6m$ B. $6m(m-n)$ C. $\dfrac{1}{6(m-n)}$ D. $\dfrac{1}{6m(m-n)}$ 10._____

11. Find $\dfrac{3x}{2x+1} - \dfrac{5x}{2x+1}$.

A. 1 B. $-\dfrac{2x}{2x+1}$ C. -1 D. $-\dfrac{8x}{2x+1}$ 11._____

12. Find $\dfrac{a}{a+4} + \dfrac{4}{a+4}$.

A. $\dfrac{a}{4}$ B. $\dfrac{4}{a}$ C. $\dfrac{1}{(a+4)(a+4)}$ D. 1 12._____

13. Find $\dfrac{7}{6a^2} - \dfrac{5}{3a}$.

A. $-\dfrac{1}{2a}$ B. $\dfrac{1}{2a}$ C. $\dfrac{7-10a}{6a^2}$ D. $\dfrac{7-5a}{3a^2}$ 13._____

14. Find $\dfrac{6}{m+3} + \dfrac{8}{m+2}$.

A. $\dfrac{14m+36}{(m+3)(m+2)}$ B. $5m+13$ C. $\dfrac{14}{(m+3)(m+2)}$ D. $\dfrac{14}{m+5}$ 14._____

15. Find $\dfrac{x}{2x+4} + \dfrac{1}{x+2}$.

A. $\dfrac{1}{2}$ B. $\dfrac{x+1}{2x+4}$ C. $\dfrac{x}{2x+4}$ D. 2 15._____

16. Solve $\dfrac{3}{x} + 4 = \dfrac{1}{2x}$.

A. $\dfrac{5}{8}$ B. $\dfrac{7}{8}$ C. 3 D. $-\dfrac{5}{8}$ 16._____

17. Solve $\dfrac{4}{x+1} + \dfrac{3}{5} = \dfrac{4}{x+1}$.

A. 1 B. $\varnothing$ C. 0 D. 4 17._____

Name _____

Rational Expressions Unit Review 2

Directions: Show your work neatly on another sheet of paper.

1. Simplify $\dfrac{m^2 - 3m - 18}{m^2 - 2m - 24}$.

   A. $\dfrac{m + 3}{m + 4}$ B. $\dfrac{3}{4}$ C. $\dfrac{m + 6}{m - 6}$ D. -1   1. _____

2. Simplify $\dfrac{3x^2 - 13x - 10}{x^2 - 3x - 10}$.

   A. 3   B. -13   C. $\dfrac{3x + 2}{x + 2}$ D. $\dfrac{x + 2}{3x + 2}$ 2. _____

3. Find $\dfrac{4a^2b}{5c^3} \cdot \dfrac{10c^5}{8ab^3}$.

   A. $\dfrac{2ac^2}{b^2}$ B. $\dfrac{ac^2}{b^2}$ C. $\dfrac{ac^2}{2b^2}$ D. $\dfrac{c^2}{b^2}$ 3. _____

4. What are the excluded values of "p" in $\dfrac{p - 4}{p^2 - 16}$?

   A. $p \neq -4, 4$ B. $p \neq 4$ C. $p \neq 16$ D. $p \neq -4$ 4. _____

5. What are the excluded values of "a" in $\dfrac{2a^2 + 7a - 15}{a^2 - a - 12}$?

   A. $a \neq -3, 4$ B. $a \neq -4, 3$ C. $a \neq -5, \dfrac{3}{2}$ D. $a \neq -\dfrac{3}{2}, 5$ 5. _____

6. Find $\dfrac{m^2 - 4}{3} \cdot \dfrac{6}{(m + 2)^2}$.

   A. $\dfrac{m - 2}{m + 2}$ B. 2   C. -2   D. $\dfrac{2(m - 2)}{(m + 2)}$ 6. _____

7. Find $\dfrac{4x + 8}{4x + 4} \div \dfrac{2x + 4}{x^2 - 1}$.

   A. $x - 1$ B. $\dfrac{x - 1}{2}$ C. $\dfrac{1}{2}$ D. $\dfrac{x + 2}{x + 1}$ 7. _____

8. Find $\dfrac{8p^3}{12m^3n} \cdot \dfrac{6mn^2}{4p}$.

   A. $\dfrac{p^2n}{2m^2}$ B. $\dfrac{2p^2n}{m^2}$ C. $\dfrac{2p^2}{m^2}$ D. $\dfrac{p^2n}{m^2}$ 8. _____

Rational Expressions Unit Review 2 *(cont.)*

9. Find $\dfrac{3x-9}{x^2-9} \div \dfrac{x^2+2x-15}{x^2-x-12}$.

   A. $\dfrac{3(x-4)}{(x-3)(x+5)}$ B. $\dfrac{3(x-4)}{(x+5)}$ C. $\dfrac{x-4}{x+5}$ D. $\dfrac{3(x-4)}{x-3}$ 9._____

10. Find $\dfrac{8m^3-8m}{8m^2+8m} \cdot \dfrac{m^2-1}{m+1}$.

    A. 1   B. 0   C. $m+1$ D. $(m-1)^2$ 10._____

11. Find $\dfrac{4x}{3x+1} - \dfrac{6x-2}{3x+1}$.

    A. $\dfrac{-2x-2}{3x+1}$ B. $\dfrac{-2x+8}{3x+1}$ C. $\dfrac{-2x+2}{(3x+1)}$ D. $4x+5$ 11._____

12. Find $\dfrac{2a}{a+4} + \dfrac{8}{a+4}$.

    A. $\dfrac{10a}{a+4}$ B. $\dfrac{2a+8}{(a+4)(a+4)}$ C. 2   D. 4   12._____

13. Find $\dfrac{3a}{6a^2} - \dfrac{6}{3a}$.

    A. $-\dfrac{3}{2a}$ B. $-\dfrac{3}{a}$ C. $-3a$ D. $\dfrac{-3}{2}$ 13._____

14. Find $\dfrac{6}{m+2} + \dfrac{2}{m+4}$.

    A. $\dfrac{8}{(m+2)(m+4)}$ B. $\dfrac{8}{m+2}$ C. $\dfrac{8m+6}{m^2+6m+8}$ D. $\dfrac{8m+28}{m^2+6m+8}$ 14._____

15. Find $\dfrac{3x}{3x+12} + \dfrac{4}{x+4}$.

    A. 0   B. 1   C. $x+3$ D. $\dfrac{3x+4}{3x+12}$ 15._____

16. Solve $\dfrac{4}{p} - 6 = \dfrac{1}{2p}$.

    A. $\dfrac{7}{12}$ B. $\dfrac{3}{4}$ C. $-\dfrac{3}{4}$ D. $-\dfrac{7}{12}$ 16._____

17. Solve $\dfrac{6}{m+1} + \dfrac{4}{3} = \dfrac{2}{m+1}$.

    A. 4   B. $-\dfrac{13}{4}$ C. -8 D. -4 17._____

Name _____

Algebra I Second Semester Exam Review

Directions: Show your work.

1. Joseph has a new job at Radio Hut. The manager calculates his total amount of pay, $f(x)$, for the month according to the function

    $$f(x) = 1,200 + 25(x - 15)$$

    where $x > 15$ units sold. The best interpretation for this function is that he earns _____.

    A. $25 per hour plus $15 per unit sold.
    B. $1,200 per month plus $15 per hour.
    C. $1,200 per month plus $15 per unit sold.
    D. $1,200 per month plus $25 for every unit sold over 15 units in a one-month period.

2. If the area of a rectangle is $x^2 + 3x - 18$, find the perimeter.

    A. $10x + 4$
    B. $4x + 6$
    C. $2x + 3$
    D. $8x + 12$

3. Jackie bought 5 snails for her aquarium. The snail population will double every month. The equation $s = 5 \cdot 2^x$ shows the total number of snails, "s," after "x" months.
    At this rate, how many snails will Jackie have after 3 months?

    A. 40
    B. 50
    C. 30
    D. 20

4. Which equation describes the data in the table?

    A. $y = x + 5$
    B. $y = 2x + 3$
    C. $y = -4x - 1$
    D. $y = -3x + 1$

x	y
−1	4
0	1
1	−2
2	−5

Algebra I Second Semester Exam Review *(cont.)*

5. Use the rectangle modeled below to answer the following question.

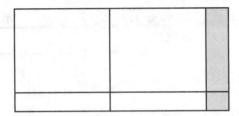

What is the area of the rectangle in terms of "x"?

A. $2x^2$

B. $2x^2 + x + 1$

C. $2x^2 + x - 1$

D. $2x^2 + 3x - 1$

6. Rory and Scott want to determine the height of the flagpole in front of their high school. Rory found that Scott is 74 inches tall and casts a shadow 104 inches long. How tall is the flagpole in front of the school if its shadow is 464 inches long?
(Find the measurement to the nearest inch.)

A. 330 inches

B. 240 inches

C. 524 inches

D. 652 inches

7. Rachel has a poster with a length 4 inches greater than its width. A frame 2 inches wide will be placed around the poster. The area of the poster and frame together is 672 square inches. Which equation could be used to find the width "x" of the poster?

A. $(x + 4)(x + 8) = 672$

B. $x(x + 4) = 672$

C. $(x + 2)(x + 6) = 672$

D. $x^2 + 12 = 672$

Algebra I Second Semester Exam Review (cont.)

8. The perimeter of a rectangle is 80 meters. The length is 14 less than twice the width. Which system could be used to find the dimensions?

    A. $2l + 2w = 80$
       $l = 14 - 2w$

    B. $l + w = 80$
       $l = 14 - 2w$

    C. $2l + 2w = 80$
       $l = 2w - 14$

    D. $l + w = 80$
       $l = 2w - 14$

9. Manny collected $55 from his baseball team to buy pizza and soft drinks. Each pizza costs $7. He bought 6 bottles of soft drinks at $1.89 per bottle. Which inequality best describes the number of pizzas, "p," that Manny can buy if the most he can spend is $55?

    A. $6p + 7(1.89) \le 55$

    B. $7p + 6(1.89) \le 55$

    C. $55 + 7p \ge 6(1.89)$

    D. $7p + 6(1.89) \ge 55$

10. Mr. Smith rented a car for weeklong vacation. The rental car charge is $55 for the week plus $0.10 per mile. If "x" represents the number of miles driven, which inequality could be used to find the number of miles he can drive the car if he wants to spend no more than $125, not including tax?

    A. $55 + .10x \ge 125$

    B. $.10x - 55 \le 125$

    C. $125 - .10x + 55 \ge 180$

    D. $55 + .10x \le 125$

11. The Snack Shack stocks 5 candy bars for every 8 bags of chips. If the manager counts an inventory of 80 candy bars, what is the total number of snacks in the store?

    A. 225 snacks

    B. 128 snacks

    C. 208 snacks

    D. 300 snacks

Algebra I Second Semester Exam Review *(cont.)*

12. What is the domain of the function at the right?

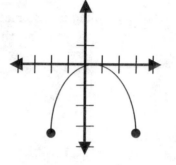

    A. $2 \leq x \leq 3$

    B. $-2 \leq x \leq 2$

    C. $2 \leq x \leq -2$

    D. $-2 \leq x \leq 3$

13. The area of a sandbox at a city park is 60 square feet. The length is 4 feet more than the width. Which equation could you use to help find the length of the sandbox?

    A. $w(w + 4) = 60$

    B. $2w + 8 = 60$

    C. $4w + 16 = 60$

    D. $(w + 4) - w = 60$

14. Reggie received a 2% commission on the sale of a new motorcycle. If the motorcycle costs $5,500, how much was his commission?

    A. $110

    B. $2,135

    C. $300

    D. $705

15. If the area of a circle is 49π cm^2, find the radius of the circle.

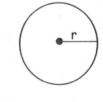

    A. 49 cm

    B. 14 cm

    C. 7 cm

    D. 8 cm

16. Which inequality describes the graph to the right?

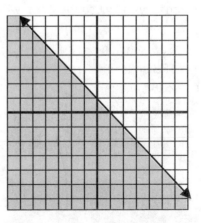

    A. $y - x \leq 1$

    B. $x + y \leq 1$

    C. $x - y \leq 1$

    D. $x - y \geq 1$

Algebra I Second Semester Exam Review (cont.)

17. Which graph below best represents the solution to the inequality?

$$-3w + 5 \geq 20$$

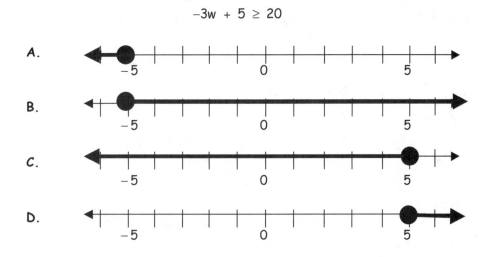

A.

B.

C.

D.

18. The graph of a line is shown below.

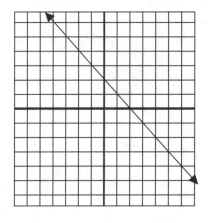

Find the equation of a second line by multiplying the slope by −1 and adding −3 to the y-intercept.

A. $y = -3x - 2$
B. $y = -x - 1$
C. $y = -3x + 1$
D. $y = x - 1$

19. The graph of the function $y = 4x - 1$ is shown below. Which equation best describes a line parallel to the graph of $y = 4x - 1$?

A. $y = -4x + 3$ C. $y = 2x - 1$

B. $y = 4x + 2$ D. $y = \frac{1}{4}x - 1$

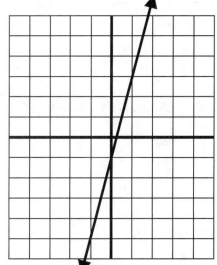

Algebra I Second Semester Exam Review *(cont.)*

20. The graph below shows the amount Karie will earn each day if she has a salary of $10 per day plus $3 per hour.

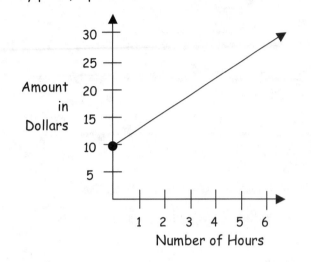

The equation is m = 3h + 10, where "m" is the amount in dollars and "h" is the number of hours worked. Which graph best represents the amount Karie will earn each day if she has a salary of $10 per day plus $5 per hour?

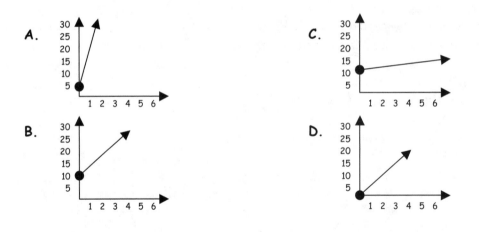

21. Beatrice is using a cake recipe that calls for $\frac{1}{4}$ cup of oil. Beatrice has $3\frac{1}{2}$ cups of oil. How many cakes can she make?

    A. 14 cakes

    B. 12 cakes

    C. 8 cakes

    D. 10 cakes

Algebra I Second Semester Exam Review *(cont.)*

22. The graph below shows the charge for a cell phone at a rate of 5 cents a minute.

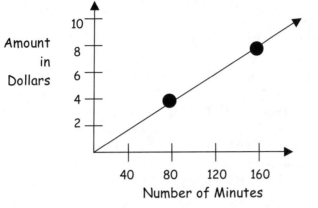

Using this information, how much would it cost if the cell phone had been used for 300 minutes?

   A. $15
   B. $20
   C. $12
   D. $18

23. Sam has a tree house that overlooks a lake. He wants to use a rope and pulley to get from the tree house to the lake as shown in the drawing below.

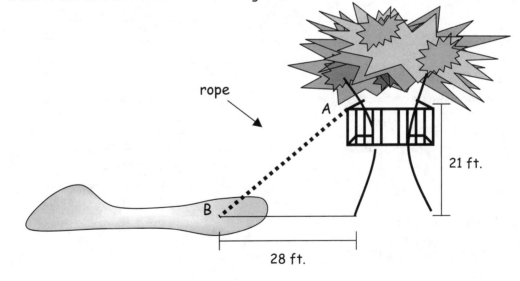

What is the distance from point A, where the rope is attached to the tree house, to point B, where the rope is attached to a stake in the lake?

   A. 612.5 ft.
   B. 30 ft.
   C. 35 ft.
   D. 1,225 ft.

Teacher Created Materials
PUBLISHING

Algebra I Second Semester Exam Review (cont.)

24. A part of the graph of the equation $y = -2x^2 + 4x + 3$ is shown on the coordinate grid.

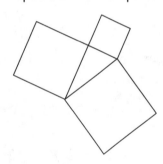

Between which two integers will the graph again cross the x-axis?
A. Between 0 and −1
B. Between −1 and −2
C. Between −2 and −3
D. Between 0 and 1

25. The sides of squares can be used to form triangles. The area of the squares that form right triangles have a special relationship.

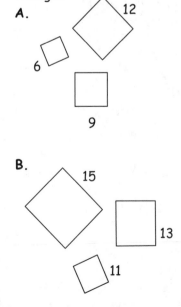

Use the lengths of the sides of the squares to determine which set of squares could form a right triangle.
A. 12, 6, 9

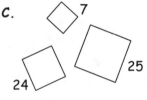

C. 7, 24, 25

B. 15, 13, 11

D. 4.5, 2.5, 8.5

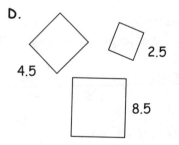

Algebra I Second Semester Exam Review (cont.)

26. $\dfrac{3n^2 - 48}{n^2 + 7n + 12}$

    A. $\dfrac{3(n+4)}{(n-3)}$ **B.** $\dfrac{3(n-3)}{(n+3)}$ **C.** $\dfrac{3(n-4)}{(n+3)}$ **D.** $\dfrac{(3n-4)(n+4)}{(n+3)}$

27. $\dfrac{m+1}{4m-1} \cdot \dfrac{16m^2 - 1}{m^2 + m}$

    A. $\dfrac{4m-1}{m}$ **B.** $\dfrac{4m+1}{m}$ **C.** $4m+1$ **D.** $4m-1$

28. $\dfrac{p^2 + 5p + 6}{p+1} \div \dfrac{p+3}{p^2 + 5p + 4}$

    A. $\dfrac{p+3}{p+1}$ **B.** $\dfrac{p+4}{p+3}$ **C.** $p+2$ **D.** $(p+2)(p+4)$

29. $\dfrac{8x}{x+2} - \dfrac{6x-4}{x+2}$

    A. $\dfrac{6x}{x+2}$ **B.** $2x+4$ **C.** $\dfrac{2(x-2)}{(x+2)}$ **D.** 2

30. $\dfrac{2}{n} - \dfrac{8}{n^2} = -1$

    A. $-4, 2$ **B.** $4, -2$ **C.** $2, 8$ **D.** $3, -4$

Name _____

Practice Using the Home Screen Method

Directions: Check the following answers on the Home Screen using the Home Screen method. Place a check beside the answers that are correct.

1. $132{,}000 = \boxed{1.32 \times 10^5}$

2. $1.4 \times 10^{-3} = \boxed{.00014}$

3. Use the Pythagorean theorem, $a^2 + b^2 = c^2$, with the following values, $a = 7; b = 24; c = 25$, to solve the problem below.

> In the figures below, the sides of squares can be used to form triangles. The areas of the squares that form right triangles have a special relationship.
>
> Using the given lengths of the sides of the squares, can the set of squares form a right triangle? Explain your answer.

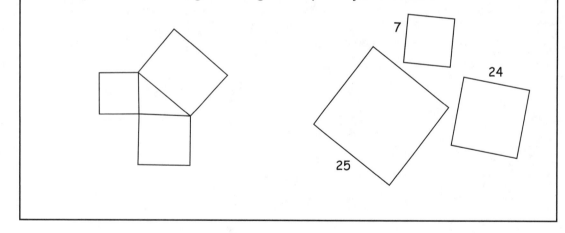

4. $(x + 2)(x - 3) = \boxed{x^2 - x - 6}$

5. $2x^2 - 7x + 5 = \boxed{(2x + 5)\,(x + 1)}$

Name _____

Practice Using the Store Before Method

Directions: Check the following solutions by storing your answer on the Home Screen using the Store Before method. Place a check beside each answer that is correct.

1. $3(x - 2) = 18$ $\boxed{x = 6}$

2. $12p - 7 = -3p + 8$ $\boxed{p = 1}$

3. $x^2 - 10x = -24$ $\boxed{x = 6, 4}$

4. $a^2 + 2a = 2$ $\boxed{a = -1 \pm \sqrt{3}}$

5. $\dfrac{3}{x} + \dfrac{1}{2} = 6$ $\boxed{x = \dfrac{6}{11}}$

6. $3 + 4\sqrt{2x} = 11$ $\boxed{x = 2}$

7. $x + y = 1$ $\boxed{\begin{array}{l} x = 2 \\ y = -1 \end{array}}$
    $4x - y = 9$

8. $y = 4x + 5$ $\boxed{\begin{array}{l} x = 0 \\ y = 4 \end{array}}$
    $3x + 7y = 35$

Name _____

Practice Using the Trace Method

Directions: Check the following solutions using the Trace method. Place a check beside each answer that is correct.

1. $x^2 - 10x = -24$ $\boxed{x = 6, 4}$

2. $a^2 + 2a = 2$ $\boxed{a = -1 \pm \sqrt{3}}$

3. Find the range of $y = 2x + 4$ when the domain is {–3, 0 ,2}. $\boxed{R = \{-2, 4, 8\}}$

Teacher Created Materials
PUBLISHING

#10623—Active Algebra—Algebra I, Guided Practice Book

Name _____

Practice Using the Table Method

Directions: Use the Table method to work the following problems.

1. Which equation represents the relation given in the table below?

x	y
−2	−2
−1	0
0	2
1	4
2	6

   a. $y = -2x + 2$

   b. $y = 2x - 2$

   c. $y = 2x + 2$

   d. $y = -2x - 2$

   e.   None of the above

2. Find the range of $y = x^2 + 6x - 8$ when the domain is {**−4, −1, 2, 3**}.

3. Find the domain of $y = 3x - 1$ when the range is {**−7, −1, 5**}.

4. Find the value of x in $y = x^2 - x$ when $y = 6$.

5. Find the missing value, if $3x + y = 0$ and (**3, y**).

6. Find the missing value, if $2x - y = 7$ and (**x, −3**).

Name _____

Practice Using the Truth Table Method

Directions: Use the Truth Table method to check the following solutions. Place a check beside each answer that is correct.

1. $12p - 7 = -3p + 8$ $\boxed{p = 1}$

2. $3(x - 2) = 18$ $\boxed{x = 8}$

3. $x^2 - 10x = -24$ $\boxed{x = 6, 4}$

4. $a^2 + 3a = 2$ $\boxed{a = -1 \pm \sqrt{2}}$

5. $3 + 4\ 2x = 11$ $\boxed{x = 1}$

6. $\frac{2}{x} = \frac{\sqrt{3}}{8}$ $\boxed{x = \frac{22}{5}}$

Teacher Created Materials
PUBLISHING

Name _____

Practice Using the Graphing One-Variable Inequalities Method

Directions: Use the graphing calculator to graph the following inequalities, using the Graphing One-Variable Inequalities method. Then, graph the inequalities by hand on the number line.

1. $6x + 3 \le 9$

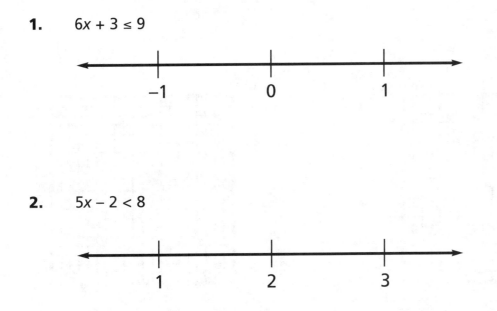

$-1 \qquad 0 \qquad 1$

2. $5x - 2 < 8$

$1 \qquad 2 \qquad 3$

Name _____

Practice Using the Graphing Two-Variable Inequalities Method

Directions: Use the graphing calculator to graph the following inequalities, and then graph them by hand on the grid below each problem.

1. $6x + 3 \leq 9$

2. $y \geq -5x + 3$

$y \leq 3x + 2$

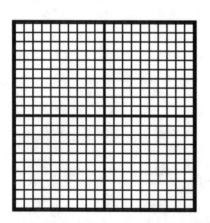

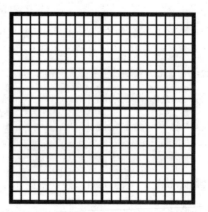

3. $y \geq 4x + 1$

4. $y > 4x - 1$

$y \leq 2x + 3$

Glossary of Algebra Terms

absolute value—the distance of a number from 0 on the number line; always a positive number

algebraic expression—any term, or combination of terms, using variables that express an operation or series of operations

associative property of addition—the sum stays the same when the grouping of addends changes; $(a + b) + c = a + (b + c)$, where a, b, and c stand for any real numbers

associative property of multiplication—the product stays the same when the grouping of factors changes; $(ab)c = a(bc)$, where a, b, and c stand for any real numbers

axis of symmetry—a line that passes through a figure so that half of the figure on one side of the line is a mirror reflection of the half on the other side of the line

base (of an exponent)—the number, or term, that is multiplied; for example, in 5^2, the base is 5

binary operation—mathematical operation in which two elements are combined to yield a single result

binomial—a polynomial with the sum or difference of two terms; for example, $5x - 3$

Boolean logic—an algebraic term indicating that when a true statement is given on a graphing calculator, a 1 is displayed, and for a false statement, a 0 is displayed

coefficient—a number in front of a variable; for example, in $5x^3 + 9x^2 - 7x + 1$, the coefficient of x^3 is 5, the coefficient of x^2 is 9, and the coefficient of x is -7

collecting like terms—when working with an expression, adding or subtracting terms that have the same variable and are raised to the same power

command—a menu item on a graphing calculator that directs the calculator to carry out a particular action

common denominator—in fractions, a number divisible by all the denominators; for example, 12 is the least common denominator of $\frac{1}{4}$ and $\frac{5}{6}$

common factor—a number that divides evenly into all the given terms; for example, 3 is a common factor of 9 and 12

commutative property of addition—the sum remains the same when the order of addends changes; $a + b = b + a$, where a and b are any real numbers.

commutative property of multiplication—the product remains the same when the order of the factors changes; $a \cdot b = b \cdot a$, where a and b are any real numbers

consecutive numbers—numbers that follow one another in order; for example, 11, 12, and 13

constant—a quantity that always stays the same

coordinate plane—the plane determined by a horizontal number line, called the x-axis, and a vertical number line, called the y-axis; the x-axis and y-axis intersect at a point called the origin; an ordered pair (x, y) of numbers represents each point in the coordinate plane

cross method—a method used to factor more difficult trinomials

denominator—a term or expression written below the fraction line; it represents the number of equal parts the whole is divided into; for example, 3 is the denominator of the fraction $\frac{2}{3}$

dependent variable—a variable in a function, whose value is affected by the value of the related independent variable

Glossary of Algebra Terms (cont.)

distributive property of multiplication—property stating that the product remains the same whether one adds two or more terms enclosed in parentheses and then multiplies the results by a factor, or multiplies each term alone by a factor and adds up the results; for example, $a(b + c) = ab + ac$

domain—the possible values for x in a function; the set of values for the independent variable of a given function

equality—a statement in which two quantities or mathematical expressions are equal; for example, $x - 8 = 12$ means that $x - 8$ must have the same value as 12

equation—a mathematical statement where the left side of the equal sign has the same value as the right

equivalent—equal in value; for example, $4 + 6$ is equivalent to $5 \cdot 2$

evaluate—to find the value of a mathematical expression; for example, when evaluating an algebraic expression for a set of given values, substitute the given values and calculate the expression

exponent—the number of times a term is multiplied by itself; for example, in 3^4, the exponent is 4

factor—an integer or term that divides into another with no remainder; for example, 7 is a factor of 21

factoring—writing a polynomial expression as a product of its factors; for example, $4x^2 - 9x - 28 = (4x + 7)(x - 4)$

formula—mathematical statement, equation, or rule using variables; for example, $A = \pi r^2$ is the formula for the area of a circle

function (of x)—a relation in which every value for the variable (x) has only one value for the variable of y; for example, the total sales are a function of the number of products sold

graph—a pictorial representation of a numerical relationship among two or more terms or sets of data; a key on a graphing calculator that displays a graph screen

greatest common factor (GCF)—the highest number that divides into all of the given numbers

identity property of addition—the sum of any real number combined with 0 is the original number; for example, $a + 0 = a$ and $0 + a = a$

identity property of multiplication—the product of any real number multiplied by 1 is the original number; for example, $a \cdot 1 = a$ and $1 \cdot a = a$

inequality—a mathematical statement that uses the symbols $<$, $>$, $\leq$, $\geq$, to compare two expressions; for example, $6 > 4$ or $x \leq 9$

integers—positive and negative whole numbers; for example, $-3, -2, -1, 0, 1, 2, 3$

inverse operations—a pair of operations that are opposite of each other and undo each other; for example, + and −

least common multiple (LCM)—the smallest number, or term, that is a multiple of all the given numbers or terms

like terms—terms that have exactly the same variables with the same corresponding exponents; for example, $3x^2$ and $4x^2$

line of best-fit—a line, segment, or ray drawn on a scatter plot that estimates the relationship between two data sets, also called a linear regression

Glossary of Algebra Terms (cont.)

linear equation—a first-degree equation with two variables whose graph is a straight line; for example, $y = x + 5$

literal equation—an equation that has two or more variables

monomial—an algebraic expression with one term that is a product of constants and multiples; for example $15a^5b^2$

numerator—the number or expression written above the fraction line; represents the number of equal parts of a total number of parts; for example, 2 is the numerator of the fraction $\frac{2}{3}$

order of operations—rules describing what order to use when evaluating expressions; parentheses, exponents, multiply/divide, add/subtract

ordered pair—a pair of numbers that describes the location of a point on a grid, given in the following order: (horizontal coordinate, vertical coordinate) or (x, y)

origin—in a coordinate plane, the intersection of the x-axis and y-axis, which is represented by the ordered pair (0, 0)

parabola—a symmetric curve that is a pictorial representation of a quadratic function or a second-degree equation; the shape resembles the letter U and can face either up, down, left, or right

parallel lines—lines that are always the same distance apart and that do not intersect; lines that have the same slope

perpendicular lines—lines that intersect at a 90-degree angle; lines that have a negative reciprocal slope

plotting—placing points on a grid or a number line

point—an exact location in space that has no length, width, or thickness

polynomial—an algebraic expression with two or more terms (monomials) that are added, subtracted, multiplied, or divided

power—another name for an exponent

proportion—an equation that states that two ratios are equal; for example, $\frac{2}{5} = \frac{8}{20}$

quadrants—the four regions of a coordinate plane that are divided by the intersection of the x-axis and y-axis; numbered counterclockwise from the upper right, I, II, III, IV

quadratic—involving expressions with variables raised to the second power or squared

quadratic equation—a polynomial equation with the variable in one or more terms raised to the second power, but no higher

quadratic formula—a formula used to calculate the solution of a quadratic equation

radical—a $\sqrt{}$ symbol that specifies that the root is to be taken; if there is no index, it means the square root

radical expression—an expression with a number or term (*radicand*) in front of a radical symbol, which is placed over a number that signifies the square root should be calculated; for example $3\sqrt{9}$

ratio—a comparison of two measures or numbers by means of division; for example, $\frac{4 \text{ cats}}{5 \text{ dogs}}$

Glossary of Algebra Terms (cont.)

rational expression—an algebraic expression that represents a quotient of two polynomials; for example, $\frac{8x}{16x^2}$

rational numbers—a number that can be expressed as the ratio of two integers; in other words, a fraction

reciprocals—two numbers that have a product of 1; for example, $\frac{3}{2}$ is the reciprocal of $\frac{2}{3}$

scatter plot—a graph with one point representing each item measured; two coordinates for each point represent two different attributes of the measured item

scientific notation—a form of writing numbers as a product of the power of 10 and a decimal number greater than or equal to one but less than 10

simplify—combine like terms and apply properties to an expression to make calculations easier

slope—the steepness of a line from left to right, which can be calculated by finding two points on the line and dividing the change in the y-values over the change in the x-values; if a line slants upward, it has a positive slope; if a line slants downward, it has a negative slope

solution—any value for a variable that makes an equation or inequality true; the answer to a problem

square root—one of the two identical factors of a given number

squared number—the product of two identical factors

substitution—replacing a variable with a number

term—each of the members of an algebraic expression that is a number, variable, product, or quotient, but not a sum or a difference; for example, $2x$, $8y^2$, 7, $9ab$

trinomial—a polynomial with three terms; for example, $3x^2 - 4x + 3$

unlike terms—terms in an algebraic expression whose variable parts are not exactly the same; for example, $4x^2$ and $4x$

variable—a symbol, usually a letter, used to represent different values

vertex—the point at which two line segments, lines, or rays meet to form an angle

whole numbers—a counting number from zero to infinity

***x*-axis**—the horizontal axis on a coordinate plane

***x*-coordinate**—the first value in the ordered pair that indicates the horizontal distance from the origin on a coordinate plane; for example, in (4, –3), 4 is the x-coordinate

***x*-intercept**—the point at which a line intersects the x-axis; for example, (5, 0)

***y*-axis**—the vertical axis on a coordinate plane

***y*-coordinate**—the second value in the ordered pair that indicates the vertical distance from the origin on a coordinate plane; for example, in (4, –3), –3 is the y-coordinate

***y*-intercept**—the point at which a line intersects the y-axis; for example, (0, 6)

zero property of multiplication—a rule stating that the product of 0 and any number equals 0

Teacher Created Materials
PUBLISHING